HARDPRESS.NET
HOME OF HARD-TO-FIND BOOKS

A Treatise on Justification
by Thomas Dutton

George Duffield A.M.

In tali nunquam lassat venatio sylva.
A.D. 1884.

Franklin

Dec.r

A
TREATISE
ON
JUSTIFICATION:

SHEWING
The Matter, Manner, Time, and Effects of it.

By the REVEREND
Mr. THOMAS DUTTON,

Late Minister in LONDON, and Author of the Discourse
on the NEW-BIRTH, and RELIGIOUS LETTERS.

It is God that justifieth.　　Rom. viii. 33.

THE THIRD EDITION.

GLASGOW:

Printed by WILLIAM SMITH,
For ARCHIBALD COUBROUGH, Bookseller; and
Sold at his Shop, above the Cross.

MDCCLXXVIII.

ADVERTISEMENT.

THE scripture doctrine of the free justification of guilty sinners, thro' the meritorious obedience and imputed righteousness of
the adorable Redeemer, received by faith, as it is
of the utmost importance in itself, so it has ever
been one of the received articles of all the reformed churches, and is still held, by all true
protestants, as one of the most essential doctrines of Christianity. It has always been the
delightful theme of every orthodox and evan-
gelical minister; and constantly yields the most
solid comfort to every sincere Christian.

Though there have been many useful and
elaborate Treatises written upon the point, by
divines of distinguished abilities, there is yet
room for more, as the subject is inexhaustible.
—The small tract now offered to the public,
needs no recommendation: the worthy author
of it was well known; and the performance,
when read, will sufficiently recommend itself,
and has already done so, to such as have per-
used it.

The author's plan in the difcourfe is fhortly his;—To confider the doctrine of the juftification of a finner, in the fight of God, in the MATTER of it, *viz.* the complete *obedience* of Jefus Chrift, exclufive of all works of the creature;—in the MANNER of it, as, with refpect to God, it is by *imputation*, and with refpect to ourfelves, by *faith*;—in the TIME of it, as it refpects the whole *body* of the *elect*, and every individual perfon of God's *chofen*;—and in the EFFECTS of it, with refpect to the SOUL, as it regards its *peace*, its *ftate*, and its *obedience*.

In this edition, the Treatife is divided into diftinct Sections, agreeable to the above plan; and to each Section there is prefixed a fcripture text, fuitable to the refpective branches of the difcourfe. With a preface and introduction, giving fome account of the author, and the work.

The editor makes no apology for the prefent publication: he has been warmly importuned to it; and the fcarcenefs of the book, with the eafy terms on which it is now offered, (not being the one half of the former price); the interefting nature of the fubject; and the clear and diftinct manner in which it is handled, will, he hopes, fufficiently excufe the attempt.

THE
PREFACE.

*A*MONG the many peculiar and interesting doctrines in the Christian system, necessary to be properly understood, there is none of greater importance than the doctrine of the justification of guilty sinners. As right notions of this important point, is of the utmost consequences to fallen men; so the scriptures of truth exhibit the most full and distinct view thereof: there we are told that guilty men are only justified in the sight of God, by having the finished righteousness of the blessed Jesus, consisting in his active and passive obedience, freely imputed, exclusive of all good works of the creature, and received by faith.

This is not only the scripture doctrine of justification, but also the doctrine of all our reformed churches; and was of such great account with our protestant reformers, that Luther said of it, ' That the church either stood or fell, as this ' doctrine was maintained, or rejected.'

The Rev. Mr. DUTTON, author of the following Treatise, on the important doctrine of Justification, was also the author of some other Tracts. We have seen his discourse concerning the NEW BIRTH, and his LETTERS on religious subjects. In these he has given uncontested proofs of his pious disposition, and thorough acquaintance with the inspired *oracles of divine truth: and it is evident, in the whole of his performances, he has studied more the edification of such of his readers, as love truth in its native dress, when stript of every human embellishment, than to gratify their vain curiosity with a flow of words which the wisdom of man teacheth.*

In the following Treatise on Justification, he has endeavoured to exhibit to his readers, a scriptural view of his subject, in the words of the Holy Ghost, comparing spiritual things with spiritual: and, undervaluing the censure of captious and ill-natured critics, who itch more after elegant diction and well turned periods, than substantial truth, he has conveyed his sentiments in language easy, intelligible, and scriptural.——And the discourse is not only doctrinal, but practical; for, while the author discovers himself to have a clear knowledge of his subject, he also displays an experimental acquaintance with the power of religion, in pointing out the comfort of saving faith, in the atonement of Christ, and its salutary influence on the renewed heart.

The plan of his discourse is plain and comprehensive. He endeavours to give his readers a distinct view of the complete atonement of our Lord Jesus Christ, as the alone justifying righteousness of guilty sinners. This he views in both its branches, consisting in his active and passive obedience. His active obedience, which lies in his full and *perfect* conformity to the whole divine law, without the least failure, either of parts or degrees of obedience, every way answerable to the dignity of his divine person as God-man *.——In his passive obedience, which consists in his giving complete satisfaction for sin, by suffering, in the human nature, all that wrath, threatened by the law, as due to elect sinners, as their surety, and enduring the infinite execution of the curse upon him in his death, to the full compensation of all the injuries done to an infinite God, by all the sins of an elect world †.——This our author proves by the most conclusive arguments, to be the alone righteousness, by which elect sinners are justified in the sight of God, exclusive of all foreseen good works, or any qualifications in the creature, previous to their justification, all such being quite insufficient to recommend a sinner to the favour of God, and have no part in that righteousness whereby the sinner is justified.

As nothing is of greater importance, or can give more satisfaction to the real saint, than to be instructed with regard to the nature of the justifying righteousness of the Lord Jesus Christ, and how this righteousness becomes his ; so, the author of the following Treatise beautifully illustrates this interesting point, from the infallible oracles of divine truth, and shews it to be by imputation on God's part ‡; For he hath made him to be

---

* Matth. v. 17, 18.   † Gal. iii. 13.   Eph. v. 2.
‡ Rom. iv. 6.   2 Cor. v. 21.

fin, [viz. *by imputation*] for us, who knew no fin, that we might be made the righteoufnefs of God in him, [viz. *by juftification and imputation:*]—*and by* believing *on our part* *. *Here our author illuftrates the nature of faving faith, fhews how it acts, and what are its proper objects.*

With regard to the time *of juftification, our author views this both as imminent and tranfient; imminent, as an act of God's will, and confequently from eternity;* God was in Chrift reconciling the world to himfelf: *tranfient, as an act which paffes upon the whole body of the elect at once, in Chrift, their reprefentative, and on every individual of God's elect, when the foul is firft enabled to believe in Chrift* †.

As nothing can be more defirable, or yield more real comfort to the true Chriftian, than to be acquainted with the fatisfactory evidences of his being juftified, the author has accordingly fhewn, in this Treatife, the effects *of juftification, as it refpects the foul's peace, its ftate, and obedience.—He has, on this part of his difcourfe, endeavoured, in the moft fcriptural manner, to fpecify the difference between the peace of a juftified foul, and that falfe peace of an unjuftified finner.*

The author, before he concludes his excellent difcourfe, propounds a particular objection againft

* Rom. x. 10. and iv. 16. iii. 22.
† Rom. i. 17. iii. 22. 26. iv. 5. x. 10. and Acts xiii. 39.

the scheme of doctrine laid down and illus-
trated, which he answers with the greatest
evidence and clearness, and shews the absur-
dity and falshood of it in the clearest point of
view, though stated with a specious appear-
ance of truth.——The discourse is concluded
with a variety of very important and useful
instructions, natively deduced from the doctrine, admirably well calculated to gladden
the hearts of sincere Christians, as well as
for the instruction of the ignorant.

Upon the whole, it will be allowed, that
the subject-matter of this excellent discourse, is
at once comprehensive, glorious, and delightful, and of all others, of the utmost importance; and that right notions of this important article, the justification of a sinner by the
blood and righteousness of Christ, tend, through
divine grace, to yield the most solid comfort
and real joy to every true Christian. It must
also be granted, that no knowledge is of e-
qual importance with that of knowing Christ,
and the way of salvation through his imputed
righteousness. Ignorance of this cardinal doctrine of our holy religion, is joined in scripture with not-submission to it; and all such,
in the issue, must be miserable souls indeed,
who are found ignorant of Christ's righte-

sin, ufness, and go about to establish a righ-
fin, oufness of their own, not submitting
of Go.mselves unto the righteousness of
tation.ift, Rom. x. 3.

our a *To promote these important ends, the
instruction of the ignorant, as well as
the establishment and consolation of the people
of God, was, no doubt, the intention of the
pious author in composing and publishing this
discourse. The* manner *in which the subject
is handled, is concise, clear, and scriptural;
and it is hoped will be found well calculated,
through the divine blessing, to answer the
great ends just now mentioned, which, there
is no reason to doubt, have already, in some
good measure, been attained by its publication.*

*That they may be farther promoted by this
new addition, and that the knowledge of Christ,
and the way of salvation through him, may
be diffused through the world, is the sincere
desire of those concerned in the publication of
it.*

GLASGOW, Oct.
24th, 1777.

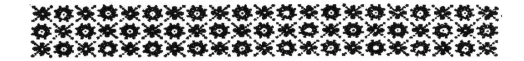

A

Treatife on Juftification.

ISAIAH xlv. 26.

In the Lord fhall the feed of Ifrael be juftified.

INTRODUCTION.

THE fcriptures of truth are the great treafury of divine knowledge; for therein, among many other precious truths, the righteoufnefs of Chrift is not only revealed, but brought near to guilty finners. The bleffed gofpel brings the moft joyful-tidings to the children of men: and as there is no other robe in which fallen men can ftand accepted, before God, but the Redeemer's juftifying righteoufnefs, this is therein faid to be *unto, and upon all that believe.* This garment of Chrift's everlafting righteoufnefs, the gofpel prefents as the alone ground of that

fir eternal falvation we enjoy by him; and
finis every way fufficient for us both to live
on, and to die in.

IN the *juftification* of a finner, in the fight
of God, I fhall confider four things
principally. As, 1. The *Matter* of it.
2. The *Manner* of it.   3. The *Time* of it.
And, 4. The *Effect* of it, with refpect to
the foul.   And then, 5. In the laft place
fhall add fomething by way of *Ufe*.   I
fhall confider each of thefe in the order
laid down.

S E C T. I.

Of the MATTER *of Juftification.*

JER. xxiii. 6.

This is the name whereby he fhall be called,
THE LORD OUR RIGHTEOUSNESS.

THE *matter* of *juftification*, or the
matter of that *righteoufnefs*, whereby a finner is made *Righteous* in the fight

of God, is firſt to be conſidered: and this, according to *the ſcriptures of truth*, is the complete *obedience of Jeſus Chriſt*, excluſive of all the creature's *works*, whether before, or after its regeneration by the Spirit of God. The complete obedience of Jeſus Chriſt, to the divine law, hath two branches, which are commonly ſtyled, his *active* and *paſſive obedience;* which conſiſt, in his fulfilling all the law's requirements, and enduring all its penalties. The righteouſneſs which God's law requires, hath two parts, *viz.* a negative part, and a poſitive part. The negative part of righteouſneſs, conſiſts, in abſtaining from, or the *not* doing of thoſe things which the law *forbids.* And the poſitive part of righteouſneſs, conſiſts, in the *doing* of thoſe things which the law *requires.* And *Sin is the tranſgreſſion of the law*, in both theſe reſpects; on which account, the law's penalty, becomes righteouſly due to every tranſgreſſor. And theſe two parts of the law's righteouſneſs, though they may be diſtinguiſhed, yet cannot be divided. For, whoever wants that conformity to the law, which it requires, is likewiſe a tranſgreſſor of it, in doing what it forbids; and whoever doth what the law forbids, wants that conformity to its precepts, which the law requires, so that they cannot be *divided*; but yet they may be *distinguished*. And the transgressor of the law, is an unrighteous person, in the eye of the law, in both these respects. And answerably, it was necessary that the righteousness of Christ should consist of two parts. As,

1. His *active* obedience, to answer to the *positive* part of the law's righteousness. And this consists, in that perfect, universal, and perpetual obedience, which he yielded to the requirements of God's holy law, both internally and externally, in heart, in lip, and in life, from his birth to his death. Whereby he gave the law its due, even all that obedience, which its extensive precepts demanded; and so fulfilled it, as to the positive part of its righteousness. For being *made of a woman, he was made under the law*, Gal. iv. 4. And *what things soever the law saith, it saith to them who are under the law*, Rom. iii. 19. Christ was under the law, and what things soever it saith, in its requirements, it said to him; and he yielded a

perfect obedience thereto, on purpose to fulfil it. Thus he says of himself, Mat. v. 17. *Think not that I am come to destroy the law or the prophets: I came not to destroy, but to fulfil.* And chap. iii. ver. 15. *Thus it becometh us to fulfil all righteousness. And he that sent me is with me,* (says our Lord;) *the Father hath not left me alone: for I do always those things that please him,* John viii. 29. He did *all* the things which God's law required; he did them *perfectly;* he did them *constantly,* or always did them, in such a manner, that God the Father was *well pleased* with his obedience. By this, he satisfied the law's requirements, and gave it *all* that it demanded: Yea, let me say, he gave it *more* than it could demand. All that the law demanded, as it was given out to *Adam,* and in him, to all his *posterity,* was no more than the perfect obedience of the creature that was under it. And this Christ yielded in his human nature; not for all *Adam's race,* but for all his *own,* whom he represented. And the obedience Christ yielded in his human nature, that nature being personally united to his divine, was the obedience of his person;

and so had an infinite worth, and glory in it; whereby he gave the law *more* than it could demand. As was foretold of him, Isa. xlii. 21. *The* LORD *is well pleas-ed for his righteousness sake; he will magnify the law, and make it honourable.* Oh how was the divine law magnified, by so great a person's being made under it! How honourable was it made by his great obedience! Let me say, the law could not have been so magnified, nor have had so much honour given it, by the most per-fect obedience of *all* the creatures, to e-ternity, as it had by the obedience of this *one* Lord Jesus! If sin had never entered, the creatures would have obeyed the law, *perfectly*, and *perpetually*. But their obedience could have risen no higher than their beings, which were but *finite;* and so the law could have had but a finite ho-nour. But the person of Christ being infinite, his obedience was such; and so the law had an infinite honour given it. O the transcendent glory of Christ's o-bedience! And how *well pleased* was *the Lord* for this *his righteousness sake!* How well pleased was he *with* this righteousness! And for this righteousness *sake,* how well pleafed was he, with all *thofe* for whom it was wrought out.   For, as our Lord, yielded a complete obedience to all the precepts of the moral law, whereby he wrought out a perfect righteoufnefs, fo he did it, not for *himfelf*, but for *us*.   As he was born for us, fo he was made under the law for us, and obeyed it for us; and thereby he wrought out a righteoufnefs for us.   He needed it not for himfelf, no; it was to cover his naked children.   All mankind had a perfect robe of moral righteoufnefs, in their reprefentative-head, Adam, while he ftood in the ftate of in-nocence.   But upon his firft fin, they loft it, and became naked; and as fuch, were expofed to the wrath of a fin-reveng-ing God.   And this was the cafe of the elect of God, as well as others, as they ftood related to the firft Adam, and con-fidered in the fall.   But thefe being of old *ordained to eternal life*, it was neceffary, that they fhould be completely righteous, that fo the law, and juftice of God, might not oppofe their enjoyment of eternal fal-vation.   And in order to make them fo, Chrift, the'fecond Adam, obeys the law perfectly for them, in fuch a manner, as

C

they, by reason of sin, were utterly incapable of. Whereby he wrought out for them a righteousness, that was every way as large, and spotless, as that which they had in their first head, Adam, before his fall: yea, in such a manner, as to make them a righteousness, that is every way answerable to his own superior glory, as the second Adam, *the Lord from heaven;* and to their transcendent relation unto him, their heavenly head, as such. The first Adam's righteousness, was a bright garment, that was every way fitted, to make creatures stand before God, with acceptance, in the enjoyment of Eden's bliss, or the natural happiness of an earthly paradisaical state; but the second Adam's righteousness, is an outshining, glorious robe, that is every way fitted, to make all those who are clothed with it, to stand before the face of God, or in his immediate presence, with the highest acceptance, in the enjoyment of the *heavenly* paradise, or *third heaven's* glory. The finite glory of the first Adam's righteousness, was changeable in itself, and might be lost; and accordingly it was: but the infinite glory of the righteousness of the second

Adam, is absolutely unchangeable in it-self, can never fade, or be loft, but en-dureth for ever. It is a *durable*, an *ever-lafting righteoufnefs*, that will abide the fame, in all the immenfe glories of it, through all the fucceffive ages of time, and to the endlefs ages of eternity. *Riches and honour are with me*, fays our Lord; *yea, durable riches and righteoufnefs*, Prov. viii. 18. And, Ifa. li. 6. *Lift up your eyes to the heavens*, fays he; *and look upon the earth beneath: for the heavens fhall va-nifh away like fmoke, and the earth fhall wax old as a garment, and they that dwell there-in, fhall die in like manner: but my falvation fhall be for ever*, (here is falvation in *this* righteoufnefs, and there is none in any other) *and my righteoufnefs. fhall not be abolifhed.* How well, then, are they dreft, who are cloathed with this glorious, un-changeable, everlafting robe! And how miferably apparelled are thofe wretched fouls, who feek to adorn themfelves with the *filthy rags* of their own *righteoufnefs*; which can never make any foul righteous in the fight of God! For, *as by one man's difobedience, many were made finners; fo, by the obedience of one, fhall many be made righ-*

C 2

teous, Rom. v. 19.   As by the *disobedience of one* man, Adam, *many,* [i. e. all his *natural posterity,*] *were made sinners;* so, by the *obedience of one, Lord Jesus Christ, shall many* [i. e. all his *spiritual seed,*] *be made righteous.* But thus much shall suffice, as to the first branch of Christ's obedience, or his active obedience to the law's requirements; whereby he makes all his *positively* righteous, to the utmost perfection, and highest glory, in the eye of the holy law, and strict justice of God.

2. The *passive* obedience of Jesus Christ, is another part of his righteousness, which was absolutely necessary to make us completely righteous in the sight of God, with respect to the *negative* part of the law's righteousness; which, as was said, consists, in the not doing of those things which the law forbids. And as we were transgressors of the law, we had done those things which were forbidden by the law; and on this account, justly deserved its penalty. And therefore it was necessary, in order to set us free from guilt, condemnation, and wrath, that he should be *made a sin-offering,* and *a curse for us,* and *die* in our stead; which, in infinite

grace, he fubmitted to. And in thefe fufferings of his, his paffive obedience confifted: he *became obedient unto death, even the death of the crofs*, Phil. ii. 8. *He was made fin for us*, 2 Cor. v. 21.; and *a curfe for us*, Gal. iii. 13.; and *died in our ftead*, 1 Pet. iii. 18. And being an infinite perfon, he was able by *himfelf*, the facrifice of himfelf, *to purge away our fins*, to overcome the curfe, to endure all that wrath which was due to us, till he had drank off that bitter cup, even to the laft drop of it; and, then, the law and juftice of God, being fully fatisfied, he was judicially *raifed from the dead:* God, the great creditor, fet him free, when he fent an *angel from heaven*, as the meffenger of juftice, to *roll away the ftone from the door of the fepulchre:* for, as he had *made peace by his blood*, fo God, as *the God of peace, brought him again from the dead, through the blood of the everlafting covenant;* and thereby did openly acquit him, as the great reprefentative of his people, in their name and room. For, as *he was delivered for our offences, fo he was raifed again for our juftification*, Rom. iv. 25. And thus by his paffive obedience, he made us completely righteous in the fight of God, and in the eye of his holy law, with refpect to the *negative* part of its righteoufnefs, or the not doing of thofe things which it forbids; and as fpotlefs, as if fin had never entered. *He loved us, and wafbed us from our fins in his own blood,* Rev. i. 5. *His blood cleanfeth us from all fin,* 1 John i. 7. And hence we are faid to be *juftified by his blood,* Rom. v. 9.; and to *have redemption through his blood, even the forgivenefs of fins, according to the riches of* the Father's *grace,* Eph. i. 7.

In as much as the law and juftice of God, being fully fatisfied by his blood, here was a way opened, in which the exceeding riches of divine grace might be extended unto us, in the forgivenefs of all our fins, with honour to all the divine perfections. In *this,* God can be *juft* in *forgiving of fins,* 1 John i. 9. And, with reverence be it fpoken, God could not forgive fin without a fatisfaction to his law and juftice, to the injury of his infinite holinefs, his unchangeable truth, and ftrict juftice. No; the glory of infinite grace, and boundlefs mercy, might not be advanced, to the eclipfing of any of the divine perfections. If it had been possible, that all the perfections of God could have been glorified, in the salvation of sinners, without the blood of Christ's cross, he had never given up the darling of his soul, unto the stroke of his justice. But it was not *possible ;* and therefore *the cup might not pass from him, without his drinking it.*——The kings of the earth, indeed, to shew their royal *grace,* do sometimes *pardon* malefactors, who are justly *condemned* by the laws of the kingdom; and herein it is true, the *clemency* of the prince is displayed, but still, the *law* suffers, and the prince's *honour* too, in relation to it. And this, because it is impossible for them to find out an *expedient,* whereby the law's *penalty* might be endured, and the *life* of the transgressor saved. But this kind of proceeding was altogether incompatible with the honour of the divine Lawgiver, and with the dignity of his righteous law. And therefore his infinite wisdom interposed, and found out a way to punish sin, and yet to *save* the sinner, to the harmonious glory of all his attributes. And this is the *great salvation,* we have by *Christ's cross.* By the cross of Chrift, we are for ever delivered from all that wrath that was due to us on account of our fin; and that in fuch a way, which makes us *fpotlefs* creatures in the eye of the law; fo that it hath nothing to charge us with, as wafhed in Chrift's blood, nor can thunder out any of its curfes againft us. For, being *wafhed* in this *fountain*, we are *white as fnow;* yea, *whiter than the fnow*, Pfal. li. 7. and have a *negative* righteoufnefs, as large as all the prohibitions of God's extenfive law. And this is an unfpeakable privilege unto us, who are finners, as confidered in ourfelves.

But then, if this *negative* righteoufnefs, which we have by the *paffive* obedience of our Lord, whereby we are freed from the law's *curfe*, was all the righteoufnefs we had, we fhould not be completely righteous, with refpect to the law's requirements, or the *pofitive* part of the law's righteoufnefs; and fo could not have a right to the *bleffings* thereof: and therefore, the *active* obedience of our Lord, or that perfect obedience which he yielded to the law's requirements, through the whole courfe of his life, is an *effential* part of his righteoufnefs, which was abfolutely neceffary to make us perfectly *righteous*, and fo fully *bleft*, according to the utmoft latitude of the law. It is this that makes us *pofitively* righteous: yea, it is this that I look upon to be, in the moft ftrict and proper fenfe, his *righteoufnefs*. It is this that makes us beautiful, glorious creatures, in the eye of God, and of his holy law; as beautiful and bright, as righteous Adam was, in his paradifaical ftate; yea, tranfcendently more beautiful and glorious: for, as was faid, that great obedience, which our Lord yielded to the divine law, was every way anfwerable to the tranfcendent dignity of his perfon, as God-man; and fo muft needs have a tranfcendency of glory in it, infinitely beyond what was poffible to be found in the moft perfect obedience of all the creatures. Does the law *require* us to love the Lord our God with all our heart, foul, and ftrength? Does it require us *always*, thus to do? We are juft *fuch* in Chrift, as it requires us to be; and have fuch a conformity thereto, that it can find no fault with, but every way approves of, and is fatisfied with. Yea, fuch a

D

conformity, that not only pays the law its *due*, and whatever it can demand of the moſt perfect creatures; but that hath a *redundancy*, an overplus, or *more* than enough in it. So that in this righteouſneſs of Chriſt, we are not only made perfectly righteous, in a law-ſenſe, according to the glory of the firſt Adam's ſtate; but ſuperlatively righteous, every way anſwerable to the ſuperior dignity of the new Adam's perſon, and the tranſcendent glory of his heavenly ſtate. And we being fore-ordained to a participation hereof, it was neceſſary that we ſhould have ſuch a righteouſneſs, that would fit us to ſtand for ever in the preſence of Jehovah, with the higheſt acceptance, as the objects of his eternal complacency.

Thus it appears, that the *active* and *paſſive* obedience of our Lord, or both theſe *branches* of his righteouſneſs, were abſolutely neceſſary, to make us completely *righteous* in the ſight of God, and of his holy law. And though theſe two parts of his obedience cannot be *divided*, yet they may be *diſtinguiſhed*: divided they cannot be, inaſmuch as that ſoul, who is *waſhed from ſin in his blood*, or by

his paſſive obedience, is alſo made *righte-*
ous by his active obedience; and whoever
is made righteous by his active obedience,
is likewiſe made *ſpotleſs* by his blood.　On
which account, the bleſſedneſs of a juſtified ſtate is ſometimes expreſſed by one
part of his righteouſneſs, and ſometimes
by the *other*.　But though they cannot
be *divided*, yet they may, and muſt be
diſtinguiſhed: foraſmuch as by his *paſſive*
obedience, we are more properly *diſcharg-*
ed from *guilt*, and *freed* from the *curſe;*
and by his *active* obedience, we are more
properly made *righteous*, and inherit the
bleſſing.　And both theſe *parts* of our
Lord's obedience, make up that *one righ-*
teouſneſs of his, whereby we are *juſtified* in
the ſight of God; or, which is the *matter*
of a ſinner's juſtification before God.

　　And as the complete *obedience* of Chriſt,
in both its *parts*, is the *matter* of *juſtifica-*
tion, or of the juſtifying righteouſneſs of
a ſinner before God; ſo it ſtands *alone*, as
ſuch, in its own comprehenſive glory,
excluſive of all the creature's *works*, whether before, or after its regeneration by
the Spirit of God.　As, Rom. iv. 6. *Even*
as David alſo deſcribeth the bleſſedneſs of the

man unto whom God imputeth righteousness without works. This righteousness, which is here said to be without works, is the obedience of Jesus Christ; which is the justifying righteousness of a sinner; and is so *complete* in itself, that nothing can be *added* to it, to make it more so. All the *works* of the creature, since the *fall*, are *imperfect;* and therefore, utterly *unfit* to be its justifying righteousness before God, either in whole, or in part. It is impossible, that an *imperfect* obedience can make the person that performs it *perfectly* righteous; and such is the infinite purity of God's nature, and the strictness of his justice, that he can accept of nothing for *righteousness*, that is not perfectly conformed to the *rule* of it, in his holy *law.* And therefore our own obedience cannot be the *whole* of our righteousness before God: nor can it be any *part* of it; because, that which is *wholly* imperfect, can be no *part* of perfection.

The best moral performances, that a person is capable of, while in an *unregenerate* state, fall far short of that perfect *righteousness* which the law requires; and therefore cannot be pleasing unto God, and accepted by him as fuch; and fo they cannot make the perfon acceptable in his fight, that performs them. Whence it is, that *they that are in the flefh*, (or in a ftate of unregeneracy) *cannot pleafe God*, Rom. viii. 8. *For without faith it is impoffible to pleafe him*, Heb. xi. 6. The chief *end* of every natural man, in doing good works, is to make himfelf *righteous* in the fight of God; and as he brings his own righteoufnefs to make him *accepted*, which falls fo far fhort of what God's law *requires*, it is impoffible that he fhould be *pleafing* to him, or *juftified* by him. So that the works of the creature, while in an unregenerate ftate, can be no part of that righteoufnefs, which makes a finner juft in the fight of God.

And as for thofe *works* of the creature, which are done after it is *born* from above, though they are indeed pleafing, and acceptable unto God, by Chrift, in point of filial *obedience*, yet not in point of juftifying *righteoufnefs*: nor doth fuch a foul perform them for that *end*. No; the foul that is born again, that has faith in Jefus, brings nothing for its *acceptance* with God, and *juftification* in his fight, but the *righteoufnefs* of Chrift: and with *this* God the Father is fo well pleafed, as it anfwers the glorious perfections of his nature, and all the requirements of his holy law, that he cannot but accept fuch a foul; and pronounce it righteous, to the utmoft perfection, in that glorious righteoufnefs its faith lays hold of, and pleads before him. Thus its *perfon* is accepted: and where God accepts the perfon, he accepts the *works* of that perfon; as Gen. iv. 4. *And the* LORD *had refpect unto Abel, and to his offering.* Firft to Abel's *perfon,* and then to his *offering.* And the reafon why God had refpect unto him, and to his offering, was becaufe he had *faith* in the *Meffiah,* who was to come; and looked for all his acceptance with God, in *Chrift,* the promifed *feed.* As, Heb. xi. 4. *By faith Abel offered unto God a more excellent facrifice than Cain.* His *faith* brought *Chrift,* typified out in that offering, for the acceptance of his *perfon,* in point of *righteoufnefs,* with God; and that *facrifice,* to be accepted by Chrift, in point of filial *obedience:* and fo both found the higheft acceptance with God. And thus all the good works of the new-born, being done in faith, are acceptable unto God, by Chrift, but not in point of righteoufnefs; nor do they perform them for that end. The good works of a *regenerate* perfon are indeed of a more excellent *kind*, than can poffibly be performed by any natural man; inafmuch as they fpring from a principle of true love to God in the heart, have an higher conformity to the perfect rule of his holy law, and the end of them is the glory of God in Chrift. But yet, they are not without *fin*; they have much imperfection in them, and need wafhing in the blood of Chrift, in order to their acceptance with God, in point of obedience. And being thus imperfect in themfelves, they can be no part of that perfect righteoufnefs, which is the matter of a finner's juftification in the fight of God.

Thus it appears, that all the *works* of the creature, both in a regenerate, as well as in an unregenerate ftate, are altogether *unfit* to be the *Matter* of its *righteoufnefs* before God; and therefore muft needs ftand excluded from being any *part* thereof.

Befides, it was not becoming the infinite wisdom of Jehovah, to *appoint* any other obedience, for a justifying righteousness, than that which is absolutely perfect, which his holy law can approve of, and his strict justice accept; and accordingly, he hath *appointed* no other. And on this account also, all the *works* of the creature, stand excluded from being any part of its justifying righteousness. As they are altogether unfit, in themselves, to be the matter of it; so they were never *appointed* for this end. No; God hath *appointed* the obedience of his Son, to be the only justifying righteousness of a sinner; and this, as was said, is so complete in itself, that nothing can be added to it, to make its glory more full.

It is impossible, that our *imperfect* obedience should make Christ's more *perfect:* yea, was ours absolutely *perfect*, yet could it add no *perfection* to his. Christ's righteousness, has all perfections in it, both created and uncreated! And what can be added to that which is infinite? and such is the glory of Christ's righteousness! Would it not then be a disgrace to this full, this glorious robe, to tack any part of the creature's obedience to it, was it ever so *perfect?* How much more then is it so, to join our *imperfect* obedience, the filthy rags of a sinner's righteousness, to the spotless obedience, the infinitely glorious righteousness of the Son of God! Would it not be a disgrace to the creature-*sun,* to pretend to set a *candle* by its bright body, to make its light more *glorious?* Much more is it so to Christ, *the sun of righteousness,* to pretend to join the dim *light* of our obedience with his, as if this could add to its infinite *glory!* No, no; let Christ stand *alone,* in that exalted sphere, where his Father has placed him, and for ever shine forth in the peculiar glory of his own great name, THE LORD OUR RIGHTEOUSNESS! while all the innumerable multitude of the saved ones, for ever bow down, with the deepest adoration; rejoicing to be made perfectly glorious, and everlastingly blessed, by the resplendent rays of his infinite brightness cast upon them! while wondering angels assist the joy, and join the praise, to the endless ages of a blest eternity!

But stay, my soul, thou art yet in the body; and must wait a while, for the

E

glory of that bright day, when, in heavenly raptures, and endlefs praifes, thou
wilt fing the *Lamb's new fong;* proclaim-
ing him *worthy* to have all the *glory* of
thy *falvation,* who has *loved thee, and
wafhed thee from thy fins in his own blood;*
and made thee fplendidly glorious, by
the refulgent rays of his own infinite righteoufnefs! which he hath caft upon thee,
and with which he furrounds thee! And
mean while, though thou art overfpread
with fin, death, and darknefs in thy felf;
yet lift up thy head, rejoice in thy Saviour,
and praife THE LORD THY RIGHTEOUSNESS,
to the utmoft of thy prefent ability, and
thy little ftrength; and humbly make thy
boaft in him all the *day* long; even all
this fhort fpace of thy mortal life, until
the days of eternity come on; and *then,*
thou fhalt *fee him as he is,* and praife him
as thou wouldeft, in thofe heights of
glory and blifs, which are yet unknown!
in that mount of vifion, from whence
thou fhalt never come down!——But, to
return from this digreffion.

The obedience of Chrift, as the juftifying righteoufnefs of a finner, being fo
perfect in itfelf, that nothing can be *added*

to it, by any of the creature's *obedience*, to make its *glory* more full; yea, so perfect, that the higheſt obedience of a creature, were it poſſible that it could be joined with it, would be but a *diſgrace* to its infinite glory: what ſaint then is there, that would deſire to be found in any other righteouſneſs, for his juſtifying dreſs before God? I am ſure, to a man of them, they are all of Job's mind, who, *though he were perfect, yet would not know his ſoul; but deſpiſe his life*, Job ix. 21. He ſaw ſuch a tranſcendent glory in his Redeemer's righteouſneſs, that though his own were perfect, he would not know his ſoul; that is, he would not approve of his own obedience, as his juſtifying dreſs before God; but would deſpiſe his life, or thoſe, his ſuppoſed, perfect works, to which the law's promiſe of life is annexed; and chuſe to be found in Chriſt's righteouſneſs, for all his acceptance with God; that ſo he might enjoy that ſuperior life, glory, and bleſſedneſs, which are only to be had in and through Chriſt. And of this mind was the apoſtle Paul, Phil. iii. 7, 8, 9. He counted all his birth-privileges, and his legal performances, both before, and after his regeneration, to be *but loss and dung, for the excellency of the knowledge of Christ* ; that so he might *be found in him,* and *his righteousness,* not having on his *own.* And all the saints are of this mind; they are such *that rejoice in Christ Jesus, and have no confidence in the flesh* ; As, verse 3.

And as the complete obedience of Jesus Christ, is the matter of a sinner's justification before God, exclusive of all its own works; so, all along, throughout the whole *gospel,* it stands *opposed* to *the works of the law,* or our own *obedience* to the law; this alone, having the broad seal of heaven, the stamp of divine authority upon it for this end. And had it not been thus, there could have been no salvation for any one soul. And therefore the apostle Paul, when he professeth himself not to be *ashamed of the gospel of Christ* ; because *it is the power of God unto salvation,* Rom. i. 16. gives the righteousness of Christ, as the reason of all that salvation, which this powerful gospel brings to poor sinners, verse 17. *For therein* [i. e. in the gospel] *is the righteoufnefs of God revealed from faith to faith.*

This righteoufnefs, which is here fpoken of, is the righteoufnefs of Jefus Chrift; and it is ftyled, *the righteoufnefs of God;* 1. Becaufe, it was of God the Father's contriving, for the juftification and falvation of his people. 2. Of his appointing for that end. 3. Of his revealing. And, 4. Of his accepting.——Again, it is ftyled, *the righteoufnefs of God;* becaufe the Lord Jefus Chrift, the perfon who wrought it out, is God equal with the Father, and has all the effential perfections of the *Godhead* in him.

And thus, in all refpects, it denotes, the glory and excellency of this rightoufnefs, and the fufficiency of it, for the juftification of a finner. Thus, chap. iii. 20, 21. *Therefore by the deeds of the law there fhall no flefh be juftified in his fight; for, by the law is the knowledge of fin.* In this verfe, all the creature's obedience, ftands for ever excluded, as its juftifying righteoufnefs before God; and therefore, if there had not been a better righteoufnefs provided, there could have been no falvation for one finner. But, in the next verfe, the falvation of God revealed in the glorious gofpel, is brought in with an adverfative, a *but*. BUT *now the righ-teoufnefs of God without the law is manifeft-ed ; being witneffed by the law and the prophets.*

This righteoufnefs is faid to be *mani-fefted*, and *now* to be manifefted ; that is, by the bleffed *gofpel*, and the difpenfation thereof, which *brought life and immortality to light*, thereby, for poor finners. And this righteoufnefs of God, is faid to be *without the law ;* that is, without our o-*bedience* to the law. But though, as if the apoftle fhould fay, this righteoufnefs of God, by which a finner is juftified and faved, is altogether *without* the law, the *works* of the law, or the creatures *obedience* to it ; yet is not the *law*, hereby, fet afide, or made void, but completely *fulfilled*. It is fuch a *righteoufnefs*, that though it is not *of* the law, nor of the law's bringing to *light ;* yet now it is ma-nifefted by the *gofpel*, the *law approves* of it, as that which aufwers all its demands, and fatisfies it to the full. The law bears *witnefs* of it as current coin, that pays it all its, due, even to a mighty overplus.

And therefore, when free-grace juſtifies a ſinner, in this righteouſneſs, that perſon is pronounced righteous, as a doer of the law; for none but *the doers of the law* can be *juſtified*, Rom. ii. 13.   And as none can keep the *law* in their own perſons, and ſo cannot be juſtified by their own *obedience;* ſo thoſe who are juſtified in *Chriſt's, the righteouſneſs of the law,* is ſaid to be *fulfilled* in them, Rom. viii. 4.

And as this righteouſneſs of God, manifeſted by the goſpel, is *witneſſed* to *by the law,* as being every way ſuch that it requires; ſo likewiſe, it is no new, ſtrange thing, that was never heard of in the world, before the goſpel, as a *diſpenſation,* entered; for it is *witneſſed by the prophets.* Thus it was foretold, what the language of all that are Chriſt's ſhould be, as they came up in the ſucceſſive ages of time; who, one by one, even every one for themſelves, ſhould ſay, *In the* LORD *have I righteouſneſs,* Iſa. xlv. 24.   And thus the Lord himſelf ſpeaks concerning his people, chap. liv. 17. *No weapon that is formed againſt thee ſhall proſper; and every tongue that ſhall riſe againſt thee in judgment, ſhalt thou condemn.   This is the heritage of*

the servants of the LORD, *and their righteousness is of me, saith the* LORD.   Thus,
Isa. xlvi. 12, 13. *Hearken unto me, ye stout-
hearted, that are far from righteousness.
I bring near my righteousness; and my salvation shall not tarry.*   And, thus it was
predicted, concerning the *Messiah,* as his
peculiar work, *to finish transgression, to
make an end of sin, to make reconciliation for
iniquity, and to bring in everlasting righteousness,* Dan. ix. 24.   And, to mention
no more, *This is his name whereby he shall
be called,* THE LORD OUR RIGHTEOUSNESS,
Jer. xxiii. 6.——Thus the righteousness of
God (the complete obedience of Jesus
Christ) without the law (or exclusive of
all the creature's works) being manifested, by the gospel, is witnessed by the
law and the prophets, as the only justifying righteousness of a sinner before God.
——And so much for the first thing proposed,
viz. the *matter* of *justification.*

SECT. II.

Of the MANNER *of Justification.*

Rom. iv. 6. i. 17. x. 10.

*God imputeth righteousness without works.——
The righteousness of God is revealed from
faith to faith.——With the heart man believeth unto righteousness.*

THE *manner* of *justification* is likewise to be confidered. And this
is two-fold; and has refpect, 1. Unto
God. And, 2. Unto ourfelves.

I. With refpect unto GOD, the *manner*
of the *justification* of a finner is by *imputation.* And this ftands, in God's *reckon-
ing*, or *accounting*, and *pronouncing* of a
finner righteous, in the *righteousness* of
his Son. And thus it ftands oppofed to
a perfon's being righteous by *inhefion*, and
by his own *performances*, as Adam was
before his fall. The law of God requires
perfect righteoufnefs, both in heart and
life, in the creature that would be justi-

F

fied by it; and it can justify such an one, and no other. But since the fall, neither *Adam*, nor any of his *posterity*, were legally righteous in themselves; and so could not be justified by their own righteousness. For, in this sense, *there is none righteous*, [*i. e.* legally righteous in themselves, and by their own performances] *no not one*, Rom. iii. 10. And *therefore by the deeds of the law, no flesh can be justified in the sight of God*, ver. 20. *All have sinned, and come short of the glory of God*, ver. 23.; and so are shut up under the curse of his righteous law, aud bound over to his wrath, in the sentence thereof; and so there is no life for a sinner by the law: it cannot justify, but must condemn an unrighteous person. But the gospel reveals a righteousness of God's providing *; wherein a sinner may be perfectly righteous in the eye of his holy law and strict justice; and accordingly justified and saved unto life eternal. And this, as was said, is the righteousness of Christ, which God the Father *reckons*, or *imputes* to a poor sinner as its *own*. He puts, or placeth, Christ's righteousness to the *sinner's* account; as he put, or placed, his sin unto

* Rom. i. 16, 17.

Chrift's fcore: As 2 Cor. v. 21. *For he hath made him to be fin for us, who knew no fin; that we might be made the righteoufnefs of God in him.* Chrift knew no fin, either by inhefion, or commiffion; and yet God the Father put, or placed, the fins of his people to his account, *imputed* them unto him, and fo made him fin for us; that fo we, who know no righteoufnefs, might be made the righteoufnefs of God in him, by having his righteoufnefs put, or placed, to us as ours, and we pronounced righteous therein; even perfectly fo, merely by *imputation*. And as it was a righteous thing with God, to impute the fins of his people unto Chrift, becaufe of his voluntary undertaking for them, as their *Surety*, in the everlafting covenant, to take their debts upon himfelf, and pay them to the full; fo likewife, it is a juft, and equitable thing with God, to *impute* the righteoufnefs of his Son to his people; becaufe it was performed by him for them, as their *reprefentative*, in their room and ftead: and accordingly, he doth impute it unto them, and thereby make them juft, and pronounce them righteous in his fight. And this is the only way, whereby a finner can be made righteous before God, *viz.* by his imputing a complete righteoufnefs to it, which the foul itfelf puts not fo much as the leaft finger to the performance of; but is wholly wrought out for it by another. As Rom. iv. 6. *Even as David alfo defcribeth the bleffednefs of the man unto whom God* IMPUTETH *righteoufnefs without works.*

And as God *imputes* the righteoufnefs of his Son to poor finners, that have none in, or of themfelves, and can be *juft* in juftifying them in this way; in as much as this righteoufnefs is fuch an one, that every way anfwers the perfect purity of his nature, and righteous law, and was wrought out on purpofe for them; fo, in juftifying a finner in this way, he difplays the *exceeding riches of his grace.* It was free grace that *contrived* and *appointed* this righteoufnefs for a finner; free grace that *accepted* of it for him, when performed; and it is free grace that *imputes* it to him, puts it upon him, or makes him *righteous* therein. Hence we are faid to be *juftified freely by his grace, through the redemption that is in Chrift Jefus*, Rom. iii. 24. And to *have redemption through his blood, the forgivenefs of fins* (which is one part of juftification) *according to the riches of his grace,* Eph. i. 7.

The *matter* of juftification, or of the juftifying righteoufnefs of a finner before God, as was before obferved, is the righteoufnefs of Chrift, or his active and paffive obedience; and the *manner* of God's juftifying a finner, by the imputation of this righteoufnefs, regards both. God *imputes* the *paffive* obedience of Chrift unto the foul, or his being *obedient unto death, even the death of the crofs;* whereby he fatisfied juftice, and thereby difcharges it from all *guilt,* and freely forgives all its *fins.* And he likewife *imputes* his *active* obedience, or the obedience of Chrift's life, to the foul; whereby he *makes,* and *declares* it to be *righteous* in his fight: And in both refpects, there is the moft bright difplay of *the exceeding riches of his grace.* And therefore the righteoufnefs of Chrift, by which a finner is juftified, is faid to be a *gift,* a *free* gift, and a gift by *grace:* As Rom. v. 15, 16, 17. *But not as the offence, fo alfo is the free gift. For if through the offence of one, many be dead; much more the grace of God, and the gift by grace, which is by one man,* Jesus Christ, *hath abounded unto many. And not as it was by one that sinned, so is the gift: for the judgment was by one to condemnation; but the free gift is of many offences unto justification: for, if by one man's offence, death reigned by one; much more they which receive abundance of grace, and of the gift of righteousness, shall reign in life by one,* Jesus Christ.——Thus the manner of a sinner's justification, with respect unto God, is by imputation, or the imputation of Christ's righteousness to him, by God the Father, of the freest grace.   And,

II. With respect unto *us*, the *manner* of *justification* is by *faith*.   And here I shall shew, briefly, 1. What kind of faith, justifying faith is.   2. How this faith acts towards its proper objects.   And, 3. How, or in what respects, the justification of a sinner is by faith.   I shall begin to shew,

1*st*, What *kind* of faith, justifying faith is.   And in order hereto, shall observe, 1. What it is *not*.   And, 2. What it *is*. And,

1. Justifying faith, is not a mere *histo-*

rical faith, or a bare affent to the truth of Chrift's coming into the world to be the Saviour of men, of his dying for finners, of his rifing from the grave, and of his coming again at the laft day, to be the Judge of quick and dead. This is no more than the *devils* have, who *believe and tremble*; and no more than what thoufands may have, where the gofpel comes, and yet *die in their fins*, and perifh for ever. But,

2. Juftifying faith, is a *fpecial* faith, that is peculiar to *God's elect*; and therefore ftyled, *the faith of God's elect*, Tit. i. 1. And though this faith is called *common faith*, ver. 4.; yet this phrafe denotes no more, than that it is common to all the elect of God; and is not to be underftood, as if it was common to others, together with them. It is likewife ftyled *precious faith*, 2 Pet. i. 1. *To them that have obtained like precious faith with us.* And it is faid to be a *gift* of God's free grace, to the faved ones, Eph. ii. 8. That fame free grace, that gives them *falvation*, as *the end of their faith*, gives them *faith* as a *means* to that end. This gift of juftifying faith, fprings out of the grace of

election; and therefore it is said, Acts xiii. 48. *As many as were ordained to eternal life, believed.* And to denote the speciality of its kind, it is said to be *the faith of the operation of God, who raised Christ from the dead,* Col. ii. 12. And to be effected by the *exceeding greatness of God's power, which he wrought in Christ, when he raised him from the dead,* Eph i. 19, 20. But thus much as to the *kind* of justifying faith. I come to shew,

2*dly*, How this faith *acts* towards its proper *objects.* The objects of justifying faith are, the person of *Christ* in his death and resurrection, his blood and righteousness; and *God* the Father, in and through him, as justifying the ungodly. Christ is the *immediate* object, and God in him the *ultimate* object of this justifying faith. And how it acts towards these its objects, I am now to shew. But before I speak of its *acts,* I would just give a hint of it as it is a *principle:* for, as in nature, there must be life, before motion; so it is in grace.

Justifying faith, then, as it is a *principle,* grows not in nature's garden, is not brought into the world with us, nor acquired by human endeavours; but is wrought in the foul, by the almighty energy of the Spirit of God, at the time of regeneration. And hence, the grace of faith is reckoned up among the reft, as the *fruit of the Spirit*, Gal. v. 22. When I fay the principle of faith is wrought in the foul, by the *Spirit* of God, I intend thereby, *his* immediate *efficiency* therein; and not to exclude the *Father* and the *Son*, from this great work. No; all the three perfons in God, have a joint *efficiency* in the work of faith; and accordingly, it is ascribed to them all: fometimes to the *Father*, fometimes to the *Son*, and fometimes to the *Spirit*; becaufe all have a joint hand therein. The *Father* works it by Chrift, *Chrift* works it from the Father, and the *Spirit* works it from both. For, when the appointed time comes, that a veffel of mercy is to be filled with the life of grace; God the *Father*, the great *husbandman*, *cuts* the foul *off from the wild olive tree*, its old ftock, the firft Adam, and the old *covenant*, and ingrafts into Chrift, the fecond Adam, the *good olive tree*; and thereby brings it under the new *covenant*, and gives it a new *life*, the life of grace, from Chrift, its new and living root.　**And** *Chrift*, at the fame inftant *apprehends*, or lays hold on the foul, and fecretly unites himfelf to it; and hereby communicates the *fpirit* of grace, **and the fpiritual** *life* **of** grace unto it, out of his own fulnefs. **And the holy** *Spirit* **of God, at the fame moment, being fent from the Father and the Son, takes poffeffion of the foul for Chrift, to form his image in it; and in-ftantaneoufly gives it the** *life* **of grace, or a** *principle* **of every grace, and fo, in particular, of this grace of** *faith*, **by his own immediate** *efficiency.* **Thus this grace of faith, as a** *principle*, **is created in the foul, by** *Father*, *Son*, **and** *Spirit ;* **and, with refpect to each of the** *facred three*, **is a work of** *almightinefs.* **But as the holy** *Spirit* **is the immediate efficient hereof, fo, as I faid, this principle of faith is wrought in the foul, by** *his* **almighty e-nergy.　And this principle of faith, wrought in the foul, is a fpiritual** *ability* **to know** *Chrift*, **and** *God* **in him, to have communion with him, to receive all** *grace* **from him, and to give all glory to him.**

Hence, in its *acts*, **as it is a** *Chrift* **dif-**

cerning faith, a *foul* transforming faith, an *heart* purifying faith; fo it is a *working* faith, *it worketh by love:* it unites the foul to the objects beheld; it makes *Chrift*, and *God* in him, *precious* to the foul; it makes his promifes precious, his ordinances precious, his commandments precious, his people precious; and enables the foul to lay out itfelf for the glory of God, in all holy obedience: and while it thus walks in *wifdom's ways*, it finds them *all to be pleafantnefs, and all her paths peace.* But as I am not to fpeak of the acts of faith comprehenfively but only of thofe, which are peculiar to it, as *juftifying;* I fhall pafs over thofe of its acts, whereby it is more properly called, uniting faith, fanctifying faith, and working faith; and fhall attend to the proper acts of *juftifying* faith: for in thefe it *worketh not* at all.

Thus having hinted, how the *principle* of faith is wrought in the foul, and that it is a fpiritual *ability* to know, and obey God in Chrift; I come now to fpeak of the *acts* of this principle, as it is ftyled *juftifying* faith; or to fhew, how juftify-

G 2

• ing faith *acts* towards *Christ*, and *God* in him, its proper *objects*.

And in order to the actings of faith towards these its objects, there must be first a *revelation* of them. The *principle* of faith, as I have said, is a spiritual ability to know and obey Christ, and God in him; and the *actings* of this *principle*, towards its *objects*, differ from it, just as the *actions* of the *eye*, in *seeing* an *object*, differ from its *power* of sight; and as the *action* of the *hand*, in *receiving* a *gift*, differs from its *power* of reception. And as the *eye*, in nature, though it be ever so good, cannot *discern* an object, unless it is presented before it, in *light*, the proper *medium*, whereby it may be beheld; so, neither can the *eye* of faith see Christ, unless he is *revealed* to it, by his Spirit in his word. And as the *hand*, in nature, cannot *receive* a *gift*, unless it is exhibited to it; so neither can the *hand* of faith, *receive* Christ, unless he is *held forth* thereto, and *put into it* by his Spirit and word. And therefore, says our Lord, speaking of the holy Ghost, *he shall glorify me; for he shall receive of mine, and shall shew it unto you,* John xvi. 14.

And further, in order to the *revelation* of Chrift, (for I begin with Chrift, becaufe he is the *immediate* object of faith) the holy Spirit of God, having wrought the principle of faith, .difcovers to the foul, its own miferable and wretched ftate by nature; as being under the guilt and power of fin, the curfe of God's law, and the due defert of his eternal vengeance. And this he does, by bringing the law home to the confcience, in its purity and fpirituality; as it requires perfect, univerfal, and perpetual obedience, in heart, lip, and life; and denounceth wrath and death upon every tranfgreffor, for the leaft failure herein. Whereupon, the foul receives a full conviction of its prefent mifery, and of its utter inability to help, or deliver itfelf from it; and fo it dies unto all hope of life by the law. And having fuch a clear difcerning by faith, of the depth of its mifery, as it never before had, nor could have imagined, it cries out, as being in the greateft diftrefs, *What muft I do to be faved?*

And now, the foul being *fick*, has a fenfible *need* of the *phyfician*. And being hereby *prepared* for the revelation of Chrift, the holy Spirit *reveals* him to the soul, and sets him before the *eye* of its faith, in all his fulness, as the great Saviour, as every way suitable to its case, as a miserable sinner. And hereby he makes such an alluring display of his glory to it, that attracts the whole soul after him. And as he presents the excellency of Christ to the eye of faith, so he convinces the soul of the absolute necessity of *looking* unto him alone, for all its salvation. As it is the command of God, that a perishing sinner, made sensible of its misery, should *believe on the name of his Son Jesus Christ*; and as it is the declaration of heaven, *that there is salvation in no other,* either person, or thing, nor in any other way, than by *faith* in him; whereupon, the soul seeing the misery and damnation that will inevitably be the lot of all unbelievers, and the happiness and salvation of all those who are enabled to believe in Christ; it attempts to put forth an *act* of faith on him, for itself, being emboldened herein by the *command* of God, and encouraged hereto by the indefinite *promises* of the gospel. And though the soul feels its utter *inability* to put forth an *act* of faith on Chrift, for itſelf, by reaſon of thoſe weights which are upon it, thoſe innumerable ſins and fears which drag it downward towards deſpair; yet it is enabled ſo to do, by the *exceeding greatneſs of God's power, according to the working,* the energy, or the preſent exerting *of his mighty power, which he wrought in Chriſt, when he raiſed him from the dead, and ſet him at his own right-hand,* &c. Eph. i. 19, 20. And as the ſoul is enabled to act faith upon *Chriſt;* ſo it is upon him, as preſented in ſome *promiſe,* or declaration of the *goſpel.* For, as the *Spirit* is the revealing *agent,* and *Chriſt* the revealed *object;* ſo the *goſpel,* in the hand of the Spirit, is the revealing *light;* in which faith's *object,* being preſented, it *acts* towards him as ſuch, according to the degree of the revelation made, and aſſiſtance afforded, by that ſovereign Lord, who, as he worketh herein, *divideth to every man ſeverally as he will.*

And by the way, this ſhews the woful ignorance of thoſe perſons, who think *faith* is a light matter; and from thence are apt to ſay, What! muſt we do nothing to be ſaved, but juſt *believe?* This is an

eafy thing indeed. But, ah! miferable
fouls, how wretched is their cafe who
thus argue! This fhews them to be yet
in the gall of bitternefs, **and in the bonds of**
iniquity; that they never knew what the
pangs of the new-birth, nor foul-plunges
were: that they never experienced what
it is, for a foul to have the guilt of fin
charged home upon the confcience, to
have the curfes of the law roaring out a-
gainft it, and to be ftript naked of all
felf-righteoufnefs and ftrength; and, in
fuch a cafe and time, to be called to put
forth an act of faith on Chrift for itfelf;
and that they never knew, what power
is requifite, to enable a foul fo to do.
Will any fay it is an eafy thing to *believe?*
Aye, fay I, fo it is, with fuch a *faith*
that thoufands have, and yet *perifh.*
With fuch a *faith*, by which the foul
fhelters itfelf under the falfe *refuges* of
its own apprehended righteoufnefs and
ftrength; while it *wears its own garment,*
and *eats its own bread,* i. e. works for
life, or thinks to live upon its own earn-
ings; while it only makes mention of
Chrift, and would be *called by his name,*
a Chriftian, to *take away* its *reproach,*

Ifa. iv. 1. It is an easy thing to *believe*, with such a *faith*, that can only stand in a *calm;* but is it an *easy* thing to *believe* in a *storm?* When the storm of God's apprehended *wrath* beats vehemently against the soul; then for it, in the face of the *tempest*, to put forth an *act* of faith on Christ for *itself*, is this an *easy* thing? If it is an *easy* thing for a *dead* man to *act;* then it is an *easy* thing for an *unregenerate, unquickened* soul, to put forth an *act* of saving faith upon Christ. If it is an *easy* thing for a creature, in the utmost *weakness*, to perform *mighty acts;* then, is it an *easy* thing, even for the new-born soul, in all its felt *weakness*, to put forth an *act* of *faith* on Christ for itself, in the depth of its distress, which is such a *mighty* performance? No; this is a thing, quite out of the reach of all *creature-power*. It is indeed *easy* for a soul, that has a *principle* of saving faith wrought in it, to put forth an *act* of faith on Christ, when the *power of God* enables it thereunto; as *easy* as it is to *breathe*, when respiration is *free;* as *easy* as it is for the eye to *see* a presented object, when it has a perfection of *light*, and a plenitude of *visive* spirits; and as

H

easy as it is for the hand to *receive* a **gift** that is put into it; and for the foot to *walk* unto any designed point of the compass, when both have a fulness of *life* and *spirits* for those motions: but otherwise, to put forth an act of faith, is quite out of the reach of the creature's ability. But to go on.

It is a most certain truth, that nothing less than *omnipotence* is required to enable a soul to put forth an act of faith on Christ, according to the degree of the revelation of him made unto it. If any thing less than almightiness could work faith, the power that enables a soul to believe would never have been so aggrandized, as here, in this *Ephesian* text it is; where it is said to be *his*, *i. e.* God's power; the *greatness* of his power; and the *exceeding* greatness of his power; and that souls believe, according to his *mighty* power, and to the *working* of his mighty power, *which he wrought in Christ, when he raised him from the dead, and set him at his own right-hand in the heavenly places,* &c.

Our Lord, by the almighty power of God, had a *double* resurrection from the dead; and so have his people, in confor-

mity to him. He had firſt a reſurrection
of his ſoul, from under all that guilt,
wrath, and death which he endured for
us; when the ſufferings of his ſoul being
finiſhed, and divine juſtice, in that regard,
ſatisfied, the joys of his Father's favour,
and of his being the God of peace, both
to him and his, broke out upon his ſpirit,
like the ſun from under an eclipſe, and
raiſed him up to that life of joy, in which
he cried out, *It is finiſhed!* Whereupon
he *commended* his triumphant *Spirit* into
the *hands* of his *Father, bowed the head,
and gave up the Ghoſt.*——And again, he
had a reſurrection of his *body*, from under
the dominion of death and the grave;
when, in his whole perſon, he was openly
diſcharged from all the debts which his
people owed, and which he had taken
upon himſelf to pay; and as having done
it, was publicly juſtified, and entered upon endleſs life and glory, in their room
and ſtead.——Thus *Chriſt*, by the power of
God, had a *double* reſurrection; and ſo
have his *people:* for, by virtue of their
union with him, they have a conformity
to him.

They have firſt a reſurrection of their

fouls; when, by the mighty power of God, they are raifed up from under all guilt, wrath, and death in the confcience, unto *faith* in Jefus; whereby they receive a full difcharge from all fin, a right and title to endlefs life and glory, and enter into the prefent life of a joyful perfuafion thereof; which is the firft fruit of that full harveft of joy and glory, referved for them, when they fhall enter into life eternal.——And again, they fhall have a refurrection of their *bodies,* at Chrift's fecond coming; they fhall be openly difcharged from all fin, and publicly pronounced righteous; and as fuch, called to *inherit the kingdom which* is *prepared* for them.—— Thus the refurrection of Chrift's people, in general, bears an analogy with his; and in particular the refurrection of their *fouls,* when firft raifed up unto *faith* in him, as dying for their fins, *and raifed again for* their *juftification;* and is effected by the fame *mighty power of God, which he wrought in Chrift, when he raifed him from the dead;* according to that proportion, which was requifite to raife the head and the members.

And as the firft *actings* of faith, in the

same soul, pafs under various descriptions; such as, *looking unto Jefus*, *coming* unto Chrift, *fleeing* unto him, the *city of refuge*, *running into his name, as a ftrong tower, committing* the foul into his *hands,* and *trufting* in his *name,* for life and falvation; fo the firft *actings* of faith, in *different* fouls, may in fome meafure *vary,* while, as was faid, they believe according to the *meafure* of the revelation of Chrift, made unto them, and to the *degree* of affiftance afforded them; and yet in the main, they all *agree,* and may be fummed up in this, *viz.* The foul's believing on Chrift, for itfelf, for all life and falvation. Some fouls have clearer views of Chrift, and are enabled to believe on him more ftrongly, and others are more weak in faith: but yet all believe truly, that have a *difcerning* of Chrift, as the only Saviour, and *truft* in him alone, for all their falvation.

There were *fix cities* appointed, under the *Jewifh* ftate, to be *refuge cities;* whither the *man-flayer* might flee, and be fafe: all which typified out that fulnefs of refuge and fafety, that there is in our one Lord Jefus for perifhing finners, that flee unto him by faith, as the hope set before them in the gospel.   And as the *man-slayer*, being to *haste* for his life unto one of *the cities of refuge*, was ordered to flee unto that city which was *nearest* to him; so it is the duty and privilege of poor sinners, when they see their miserable condition, to *haste* immediately unto *Christ*, the great *Saviour;* and unto *that* in Christ, which they have the clearest *discerning* of, and so in that regard, is the *nearest* unto them; as being a suitable *relief* for that part of their *misery*, which most sensibly *affects* them.——And thus some souls, being most sensibly touched with the guilt and filth of *sin*, have a more clear revelation of the *blood of Christ*, in its excellency and suitableness, to *cleanse from all sin*, and are enabled to haste unto *this*, as the immediate *refuge* set before *them*.——Other souls are more sensible of their misery, as *naked* creatures, and have a more clear discovery of Christ, as a suitable, glorious remedy, in regard to his *righteousness;* and these are enabled to run into his name, THE LORD OUR RIGHTEOUSNESS, as the *refuge* that is *next*, or most immediate unto *them*.——And others, who have a more *general* fenfe of their mifery, have a more *general* revelation of Chrift's excellency; and are enabled to flee unto him for *refuge*, as a complete *Saviour*, that is every way fuitable to *their* cafe. And though the diftinct *actings* of faith on Chrift, in all thefe, *vary;* yet in the main they *agree*, inafmuch as it is one *Chrift*, that is believed on for juftification and life. They all flee unto Chrift for *refuge*, and fo are all *fafe;* though one flees unto him under one confideration, and another under another, according to that revelation they have of him, as fuitable to their cafe. For, though the foul's firft actings of faith on Chrift, may more peculiarly refpect fome *one* of his diftinct excellencies, than the reft, yet *all* are implyed: faith acts towards a *whole* Chrift; and thofe of his excellencies, which were not at firft fo diftinctly viewed, and *acted* towards by the foul, are afterwards more fully *difcovered*, and particularly dealt with.—Thus in *general*, juftifying faith *acts* towards Chrift its *object*.

But more *particularly;* the holy Spirit of God, as the *Spirit of wifdom and revelation*, reveals the *blood* of Chrift to a fin-

burdened foul, in its infinite all-fufficiency
to cleanfe from all fin, in fome one or o-
ther promife or declaration of the gofpel;
and enables the foul to *act* faith therein.
Thus Rom. iii. 25. *Whom God hath fet
forth to be a propitiation, through faith in
his blood.* And the particular *actings* of
juftifying faith, towards Chrift, with regard to his blood, are, 1. A *difcerning* of
its all fufficiency to take away fin. 2. An
approving of it as fuch. And, 3. An
entire *dependance* upon it, and recourfe
unto it, for all pardon and peace with
God. All which are comprehended in
that phrafe, *Faith in his blood.*

The foul that *acts* faith in Chrift's *blood*,
as on the one hand it *difcerns* the infinite
all-fufficiency thereof, to cleanfe it from all
fin; fo, on the other, it fees an utter
infufficiency in every thing elfe, in all its
prayers, tears, fufferings, *&c.* to take
away the leaft *fin*, or in the leaft-wife to
remove, either the guilt or ftain of any
of its tranfgreffions.

And as fuch a foul *approves* of the
blood of Chrift, as fufficient in itfelf to
take away fin, and as it is appointed of
God for this end; fo, it *difapproves* of the

pretended efficacy of every thing elfe for this purpofe.

Again, as fuch a foul has an entire *dependence* upon the precious *blood* of Chrift, for all its pardon and peace with God, and as it has an utter *independence* upon every thing elfe, either to procure its pardon, or make its peace; fo, it would not, for a world, *fubftitute* any thing of its own, either doings or fufferings, in the room of Chrift's *blood*, or *join* them together with it; becaufe it fees, that nothing elfe can take away *fin;* and alfo, becaufe it would not derogate from the honour of the Redeemer's *blood:* no; the foul that acts faith in Chrift's blood, falls down and adores the *Redeemer*, in the infinite all-fufficiency of his great *facrifice*, and depends upon this alone, for its juftification from all fin, in the fight of God. Faith will give none of the glory, that is due to Chrift's *blood*, as it cleanfeth from all fin, to any thing done or fuffered by the *créature;* but fets the crown upon the Redeemer's head, and proclaims the *Lamb worthy to have all the glory of wafhing his people from their fins in his own blood,* Rev. i. 5.——Thus juftifying faith *acts* towards

I

Chrift, its *object*, with regard to his *paf-five* obedience, his *blood*, according to the revealed efficacy thereof, for a full dif-charge from all fin.

Again, the Spirit of Chrift reveals to the foul, in and by the gofpel, his *active* obedience, his *righteoufnefs*, ftrictly fo call-ed; and faith *acts* towards it accordingly. Thus, Rom. i. 17. this *righteoufnefs of God* is faid to be *revealed from faith to faith.* As the righteoufnefs of Chrift is *externally* revealed in the gofpel, which is the doctrine of faith; fo likewife, it is *internally* revealed by his Spirit to the foul; or fet before the eye of its faith, in fome one or other word of the gofpel, fhining in upon the heart in the light of the Holy Ghoft. Chrift is faid to be *made of God unto us righteoufnefs, as well as re-demption,* 1 Cor. i. 30. As he is made redemption to us, both by price and power for the forgivenefs of all our fins, and for our deliverance from all enemies; fo he is made righteoufnefs to us, for the juf-tification of our perfons in the fight of God; or, for the making us pofitively righteous before God, to the utmoft per-fection: whereupon we are declared righteous, have now a title to, and fhall, ere long, inherit eternal life. So likewife, it is faid, that Chrift was *made fin for us, that we might be made the righteoufnefs of God in him,* 2 Cor. v. 21. And that it is *by the obedience of one, that many fhall be made righteous,* Rom. v. 19. And when the Spirit of Chrift takes the righteoufnefs of Chrift, and fhews it to the foul, in thefe *words,* or in any other *word* of the gofpel, he makes fuch a *revelation* of it to the mind, that it never before faw.

The foul had wont to think, that that righteoufnefs, whereby it might find acceptance with God, and be juftified before him, was fomething either *in,* or *done* by itfelf. If it had any fight of the need of Chrift's blood, to cleanfe it from fin; (as fome fight of this, a natural man is capable of, though not of that faving fight of it, which is peculiar to the new-born, upon the Spirit's revelation;) yet ftill the foul thought, that it muft endeavour to make itfelf *righteous* in the fight of God, by its own *obedience;* and that for this end it muft do good works. But when the Spirit fhews the righteoufnefs of Chrift,

to the faith of any foul, it is quite of a-
nother mind.   Now, the foul fees, that
that righteoufnefs, which alone can make
a finner juft before God, is only *in the*
LORD; *i. e.* in the Lord Jefus, as the
reprefenting head of his people.   It fees,
that CHRIST is *made unto us righteoufnefs ;*
that it is in HIM *we are made the. righte-*
oufnefs of God; and that, it is by HIS *obe-*
dience, that many fhall be made righteous.
And as by this revelation of the Spirit,
the foul fees the righteoufnefs of Chrift,
in its reality, and alfo in its beauty, fulnefs, excellency, and glory; fo, by faith,
it *acts* towards it for juftification.   As
this righteoufnefs is *revealed to faith;* fo
faith *acts* towards this *righteoufnefs*, or towards *Chrift*, with regard to his *righteouf-*
nefs;   1. By *looking* unto it.   2. By *re-*
ceiving, or embracing of it.   And, 3. By
depending upon this alone, for its only
juftifying righteoufnefs before God.

As the righteoufnefs of Chrift is revealed, in the gofpel, unto all nations for
the obedience of faith; and revealed, by
the Spirit, unto all thofe who have faith
wrought in their hearts: fo faith *acts* towards this *righteoufnefs*, by *fubmitting* to

it. As is plainly implyed, in what is afferted concerning unbelievers, that *they, being ignorant of God's righteoufnefs, go a-bout to eftablifh their own righteoufnefs, and have not fubmitted* themfelves unto *the righteoufnefs of God,* Rom. x. 3. If this is the character of an unbeliever, that he is fuch an one, that doth not *fubmit* to this righteoufnefs of God; then the character of a believer muft be juft the *'reverfe;* and the foul that *acts* faith, in fubmitting to this righteoufnefs, *looks* unto this alone, for its juftification in the fight of God.

As poor finners are called to *look unto Jefus* alone, for all that fulnefs of *falvation* that is in him; fo, in particular, they are called to look unto him, as THE LORD OUR RIGHTEOUSNESS; and that when they are far from righteoufnefs, or have none at all of their own to recommend them to God: As, Ifa. xlv. 22. *Look unto me, and be ye faved, all the ends of the earth.* And, chap. xlvi. 12, 13. *Hearken unto me, ye ftout-hearted, that are far from righteoufnefs: I bring near my righteoufnefs.* It is as if the Lord fhould fay, ' Hear ye ftout-
' hearted fouls, that, in the pride of your

' spirits, have refused subjection to my
' righteousness, and have gone about
' making yourselves righteous, by the
' works of your own hands, which yet
' leave you in a state that is far from
' righteousness; I bring near my righte-
' ousness, I have a righteousness for you,
' that you never thought of; a complete
' glorious robe, of my own working out,
' in which there is a fulness of salvation
' for you: look therefore, upon this *my*
' righteousness, and be ye saved.' And
accordingly, the soul that believeth, *looks*
away from all its own righteousness, as
being fully convinced of the vanity of
looking for salvation from thence; and
looks unto the Redeemer's righteousness,
and to that alone, as being infinitely sufficient to justify and save it. And the
language of such a soul, when it comes
unto Christ for justification of life, is the
same with that of the church, Jer. iii. 23.
Truly in vain is salvation hoped for from the
hills, and from the multitude of mountains;
(from the works of our own hands, which
were once high as mountains, in our e-
steem, for security) *Truly in the* LORD *our*
God is the salvation of Israel. And thus,

Hof. xiv. 3. *Afhur fhall not fave us, we will not ride upon horfes, neither will we fay any more to the work of our hands, Ye are our gods;* (our deliverers, to whom we look for falvation.) *For in thee the fatherlefs find mercy:* it is as if they fhould fay, we are fuch miferable fouls, that cannot fave ourfelves, and have none to provide us either bread or *cloathing*, in a fpiritual refpect; but thou haft *all* we want: we come to thee therefore, in our ftarving, *naked* condition; and *look* to thee, for that bread, that *cloathing* which thou haft provided; for in thee we fhall find all the mercy we can want, unto eternal life.——Thus, a poor foul, when ftript *naked* of all its own *righteoufnefs*, *looks* by faith unto Chrift's, as its only juftifying robe. And the eye of a believer is *fingle* towards Chrift, in this refpect; it does not look partly to *Chrift*, and partly to its own *works*, to make it righteous in the fight of God. No, Chrift commends his fpoufe, as having *doves eyes*, Song iv. 1. that look *fingly* unto *him*, her glorious *Mate*, for that royal robe of his, that *wedding-garment*, which can only fit her to ftand with him, in the heights of glory, before the face of God, with the higheft acceptance.

Again, juftifying faith *acts* towards *Chrift*, its *object*, with regard to his *righteoufnefs*, by *receiving* or embracing of it. This righteoufnefs is ftyled *a gift*, Rom. v. 17. And accordingly, the hand of faith *receives* it, as a gift of the Father's free love, to a naked finner, to make it completely righteous in his fight: for, in *giving* Chrift to the foul, he gives him in all his *fulnefs*, and fo in *this*, of his glorious *righteoufnefs*, which is infinitely full for its *juftification*. And faith *receives* Chrift, as God *gives* him; it *receives Chrift Jefus the Lord*, as the Father's *gift*, in all his fulnefs, in all his glories, and fo in this, of his being its complete *righteoufnefs* before God; and as fuch it *walks* in him, in all its approaches to the Father, as the faints are exhorted to do, Col. ii. 6. As faith's eye *looks* unto this righteoufnefs; fo faith's hand *receives* it: it brings nothing to *buy* this righteoufnefs with; nor yet doth it bring any thing to *join* with it; but merely *receives* it, in the fulnefs of its glory, and freenefs of its beftowment.

As this righteoufnefs is a royal *grant* from the throne, to *array* the *bride* of Chrift, and fo every believer, who, in itfelf, is a naked creature; fo the foul by faith *receives* it, and *puts* it on, as it were: *It puts on the Lord Jefus* as its righteoufnefs before God, enwraps itfelf herein, and adorns itfelf herewith; and hereby *makes itfelf ready for the marriage of the Lamb.* And in this fpotlefs, beauteous, glorious robe, it will appear to be made ready indeed, for the enjoyment of the marriage-glory, with its royal Bridegroom, when that happy day comes on, Rev. xix. 8. An *unbeliever*, as he has no *eye* of faith, no fpiritual ability to *fee* Chrift's righteoufnefs; fo he has no *hand* of faith, or fpiriritual ability to *receive* it. No; the *eye* of the natural man *looks* to his own works, to make him righteous: thefe he admires, bows down to, and idolatroufly fets up in the room of Chrift's righteoufnefs. And as for his *hand*, it is a *working* hand, not a *receiving* hand; it *works* for righteoufnefs, not *receives* righteoufnefs. The natural man is too proud to be beholding to free-grace, for a righteoufnefs before God, that is all of mere *gift*, and of another's working out; this he *understands* not, this he *approves* not, to this he *submits* not.   But to a *believer*, O what a glorious fight is the righte-oufnefs of Chrift, in his eye, as it is the Father's free *gift*, for the juftification of a finner!   And, with what gladnefs doth the hand of faith *receive* and embrace this gift of righteoufnefs!

And as the foul, by faith, looks to and receives this righteoufnefs; fo it *depends* upon this alone, for its juftification before God.   And therefore, the apoftle gives this defcription of believers, that they are fuch *that rejoice in Chrift Jefus, and have no confidence in the flefh*, Phil. iii. 3. As they have no confidence in the *flefh*, in their external privileges, or legal per-formances, as their righteoufnefs before God; fo they have all their confidence in *Chrift*, and his righteoufnefs, for their complete juftification in God's fight. Here they *confide*, on this they *depend;* and knowing the fulnefs, glory, and excel-lency of this righteoufnefs, appointed of God for fuch a glorious end, they do it with joy.   They rejoice in Chrift Jefus, as having an exuberant fulnefs of juftifi-

cation, life, and glory in him; even a-
bove what perfect Adam was capable of
in innocency. And as the apostle *here*
describes believers in general; so, in the
succeeding *verses*, he gives us an account
of himself in particular, with regard to
his *distrusting* every thing of his own, and
his entire *confidence* in Christ, or the *actings* of his faith towards him, in respect
to his righteousness.

Verse 4. *Though I might also have confidence in the flesh, if any other man thinketh
that he hath whereof he might trust in flesh,
I more.* It is as if he should say, ' I have
' as much of external privilege, and legal
' performance, as any of you all; and if
' these things would stand me in any
' stead, for my righteousness before God,
' I might trust in them as much as any
' man, nay, more.'

And then he proceeds, verses 5, 6. to
give a particular enumeration of his privileges and performances; *Circumcised the
eighth day,* says he; *of the stock of Israel,
of the tribe of Benjamin, an Hebrew of the
Hebrews; as touching the law a Pharisee;
concerning zeal, persecuting the church;
touching the righteousness which is in the*

law, blameless.   It is as if he should say,
‘ Come, you *Jews*, who *rest in the law,*
‘ *and make your boast of God,* and see if I
‘ am a *whit* behind you, in any of your
‘ *birth,* or *church* privileges, and *legal*
‘ performances, in which you vainly trust;
‘ or rather, whether I have not *more* of
‘ those things, than many of you can
‘ pretend to.——Are you *Hebrews,* of the
‘ seed of *Abraham,* whom God chose to
‘ be his peculiar people? *So am I.* Yea,
‘ an *Hebrew* of the *Hebrews;* I am so, both
‘ by father’s and mother’s side; which
‘ many of you cannot say.——Are you *of*
‘ *the stock of Israel,* who as a prince with
‘ God, prevailed with him for the blessing?
‘ *So am I.* And I can tell you of what
‘ *tribe* too, I am of *the tribe of Benjamin;*
‘ when many of you cannot reckon up
‘ your *genealogy.*——Were you *circumcised?*
‘ *So was I.* And that at *the eighth day*
‘ too, the precise time appointed by God;
‘ which many of you cannot say.——Have
‘ you been observers of the *law?* So
‘ have I. *As touching the law, a Pha-*
‘ *risee; of the strictest sect:* and *profited*
‘ *more in the Jews religion, than many of*
‘ *mine equals,* who profess themselves to

be *Pharisees*, of the same *sect* with me. ——Have you been strenuous *maintainers* of the *Jewish religion*, and *opposers* of all you judged innovations, and destructive of the rites and ceremonies thereof? *So have I.* I was no cold half-hearted professor, that cared not what men believed, or practised in religious matters; but was so *exceedingly zealous of the traditions of the fathers*, that in this my blind *zeal*, I even *persecuted the church of God, and verily thought I ought to do many things contrary to the name of Jesus of Nazareth;* because I judged that *Jesus*, and his *followers*, taught and practised things contrary to the law of *Moses*, and the religion *established* by God himself. *And being exceedingly mad against them, I breathed out threatenings and slaughter, haled men and women to prison; some I compelled to blaspheme, and others I persecuted even to strange cities;* so that in this regard, I was as great an *hero* as any of you all, and perhaps there is not a man among you, that has been so great a zealot as myself; *concerning zeal persecuting the church.*——And as for *the righteousness which is in the law,* take

' it in the most comprehensive sense,
' which our doctors have given of it, *I*
' *was blameless.* None could charge me
' with an unrighteous action, with any
' want of conformity to, or transgression
' of the law of God, according to that
' sense of it given by the *Rabbins;* I have
' been a person of a spotless conversation,
' of an unblemished character, *touching*
' *the righteousness which is in the law,*
' *blameless.*

Thus he drew his own picture to the
life, and presented it to them, in all the
beautiful features of his privileges and
performances, while he remained an *unbeliever.* ' And now, you *Jews,* as if he
' should say, who are fond of your own
' *righteousness,* and trust in this for your
' acceptance with God, what think you
' of such a man as I? Do not you think
' *my* righteousness was large enough to
' cover me all over, and to render me
' acceptable unto God? If any man of
' you all *think he hath whereof he might*
' *trust in the flesh, I more.* Surely I had
' righteousness enough to *vie* with you
' all, and to *outstript* many of *you.* But
' come now, you *self-righteous* creatures,

' and I will tell you how little *worth* all
' your own *righteousnefs* is, in point of
' *acceptance* with God. I once thought,
' as you now do, that I had righteousnefs
' fufficient to juftify me in the fight of
' God; but come I will tell you my *ex-*
' *perience,* how infufficient I faw the beft
' righteousnefs of a fallen creature to be,
' what little account I made of all my
' *own* righteousnefs; and what great ac-
' count I made of *Chrift*'s, when *God re-*
' *vealed his Son in me,* and wrought faith
' in my heart. You have feen me *exalt-*
' *ing* myfelf to the greateft altitude of
' that *pharifaical* perfection, I had while
' an *unbeliever;* and now you fhall fee
' me, as a *believer, laying* my *felf,* and
' all my *own* righteousnefs, down at the
' *feet* of Jefus; fhrinking into the duft,
' under a fenfe of all my own nothingnefs
' and vilenefs, before this Lord of glory,
' who is THE LORD MY RIGHTEOUSNESS;
' upon whom only I now *depend,* and in
' whom alone I now rejoice.' And fo
he turns the tables, and begins his difcourfe in the next verfes, with an adverfative, a *but.*

Verfe 7. BUT *what things were gain to*

me, thofe I counted lofs for Chrift. ' And
' now, as if he fhould fay, you poor
' fouls, that feek to be juftified by your
' works, fee how vain a thing it is to
' truft in your own *righteoufnefs*, which
' cannot endure the fiery inquifition of
' the holy *law*, and ftrict *juftice* of God.
' See how it fared with me, when God
' brought home his law in its *fpirituality*
' to my confcience; I foon found that
' none of my external privileges, and *fig-*
' *leaf* performances, could fcreen me from
' the ftorm of his avenging *wrath*. I
' then faw, that all my *goods*, I had been
' laying up for many years, and thought
' they would have *gained* me eternal life,
' were but mere *lofs;* that thefe counter-
' fits would never pafs for current coin;
' and that if I *trufted* to thefe, I muft *lofe*
' my foul for ever; and therefore, when
' my judgment was fet right, I *counted*
' them *lofs.* And as God fhewed me the
' infufficiency of my *own* righteoufnefs,
' fo likewife the all-fufficiency of *Chrift's.*
' I then faw, that *Chrift* was the only
' *gain,* that it was his *righteoufnefs* alone
' that could *deliver* me *from death,* and
' give me life; yea, I faw fuch a fuper-

' excellent glory in Chrift's righteoufnefs,
' that did infinitely exceed my *own*, had
' it been ever fo perfect; and that I muft
' *part* with my own, if ever I *had* Chrift's,
' and therefore, I freely caft all my own
' righteoufnefs *overboard*, and *counted* it
' *lofs for Chrift*, that glorious *object*, and
' thofe immenfe treafures of *gain*, I fhould
' have in *his* righteoufnefs. I *parted* with
' my own *righteoufnefs*, indeed, in point
' of *dependence*; but then it was for a
' *better*: I *caft* away all my falfely fup-
' pofed *gain*, and counted it *lofs for Chrift*;
' when once I faw the real, the infinite
' *gain*, of that glorious *object*, which I
' then *received* and *embraced*. Therefore,
' be convinced, you ignorant fouls, who
' would *eftablifh* your own *righteoufnefs*,
' that it cannot ftand you in any ftead,
' and that if ever you are faved, you muft
' have a better; that you muft have a
' righteoufnefs that *exceeds the righteoufnefs*
' *of the Scribes and Pharifees, or in no cafe*
' *you can enter into the kingdom of heaven.*
' Thus, as if he fhould fay, I have told
' you, what little *account* I made of all
' my *pharifaical* righteoufnefs, and what'
' an high *value* I had of *Chrift's*, in the

' day when God wrought *faith* in my
' heart; *I counted it loss for Christ.* And
' as I then *did* count it, so I now *do;*
' Christ has lost no *glory* in my *eye.* I will
' take all my *pharisaical* righteousness,
' while an *unbeliever,* and add to it all
' the righteousness I have wrought, since
' I *believed* in *Jesus,* and since I was an
' *apostle* of the *Lamb,* who *have laboured*
' *more abundantly than they all;* and tell
' you even now, what little *account* I
' make of all these things put together;
' and what an high *esteem,* at this time,
' I have of *Christ,* as my *justifying* dress
' before God.

Verse 8, 9. *Yea, doubtless, and I count
all things, but loss, for the excellency of the
knowledge of Christ Jesus my Lord; for whom
I have suffered the loss of all things, and
do count them but dung, that I may win
Christ, and be found in him, not having
mine own righteousness, which is of the law;
but that which is through the faith of Christ,
the righteousness which is of God by faith.*
' I put all things together, all my own
' *righteousness,* while a *Pharisee,* and since
' an *apostle,* and tell you, *I count all things*
' *but loss for Christ;* for the *knowledge of*

Chrift, for *the excellency of the knowledge of Chrift Jefus my Lord;* that glorious *object*, my faith now *deals* with, that anointed *Saviour*, whom I *adore*, as the LORD MY RIGHTEOUSNESS, in whom is all my *falvation: For him I have fuffered the lofs of all things, and do count them but dung that I may win Chrift.* I *lofe* all, to *win* all; or rather, I lofe an *all* that is *nothing*, and worfe than nothing, to gain immenfe *treafures*, an infinite *fulnefs*, a mafs of unbounded *fweetnefs*, and an eternity of *life* and *glory.* I joyfully part with *all*, for *one Chrift;* the Father's *Chrift* is infinitely *enough* for me. I caft away all my own *blemifhed* performances, for the *fpotlefs* beauty of my lovely *Lord;* and *count them but dung that I may win Chrift, and be found in him.* Oh! it is in *Chrift*, not in *myfelf*, that I would be *found*, at the awful day of judgment. It is, as *not having on mine own righteoufnefs, which is of the law;* I dare *truft* in none of my own *obedience* to God's law, which I love and ferve, as my *righteoufnefs* before God; nor would I be found in this garment, when I appear before him: *but* as hav-

' ing on *that righteousness which is through*
' *the faith of Christ, the righteousness which*
' *is of God by faith.* That *righteousness*
' which Christ has wrought out, which
' God hath appointed for the justification
' of a sinner, which faith sees, and re-
' ceives: it is this *righteousness,* I would
' be *found* in; it is upon this alone I *de-*
' *pend* for justification before God, and
'. eternal glory with him.'

Thus this great apostle gave an account
of the actings of his faith towards Christ,
with regard to his righteousness for justification.   And, as all that are justified
have the same *faith*; so it *acts,* in like
manner, towards the righteousness of Christ
for justification of life.   It is this righteousness *justifying faith looks to*; it is *this*
it *receives* and *embraces*; and upon *this*
alone it *depends*.   For, as all believers
debase their *own* righteousness; so they
exalt *Christ*'s: they set the crown upon
his head, and will for ever give him the
glory of all their *justification* before God.
As they give his *blood* all the *glory* of *cleans-*
ing them from *sin*; so they give his *righ-*
teousness all the *glory* of their *acceptance*

with God.   And thus justifying faith *acts* towards *Christ* its *object.*

In the next place, I would shew briefly, how justifying faith *acts* towards *God* its *object.*   And this, in short, is the soul's *looking* unto *God,* as *justifying,* through the blood and righteousness of his Son; and *expecting* all its justification from him, only upon the account of what Christ has done and suffered.   And in order hereto, the blessed Spirit makes a revelation of *God* to the soul, as *justifying* a poor sinner, of the freest *grace,* and yet according to the strictest justice, through the *blood* and *righteousness* of Christ; and enables the soul to *look* unto God, as so justifying for itself, even when it sees nothing but un-godliness in it; and to *receive* the justify-ing sentence of God pronounced in the word of the gospel, concerning the soul which believes in Jesus, with respect both to the *forgiveness* of its sins, and *accepta-tion* of its person; and this, merely upon the truth and faithfulness of that God, who makes the declaration.

From whence, as the soul receives that present justification given it by the gospel, into its own conscience; so it *expects* the open promulgation of this fentence, or that open juftification, which fhall be given it at the day of judgment, in the face of men and angels, when it fhall be pronounced, *Bleffed of the Father*, and called, as fuch, to *inherit the kingdom prepared for it, from the foundation of the world:* And as the foul that thus acts faith, fees it an impoffible thing, that God fhould juftify a finner in any other way, than by his free grace, through the blood and righteoufnefs of Chrift; and fo *looks* to him as juftifying, only in this way, for its own juftification and falvation; fo it likewife herein regards the *glory* of God. Such a foul brings nothing with it, but *Chrift*, for all its *acceptance* with God; nor dare plead any thing, as a moving *caufe* of its juftification and falvation, but God's free *grace;* nor doth it bring any thing of its own, to procure the divine favour; becaufe it would not eclipfe the *glory* of free grace. No; as faith *looks* for, *receives*, and *expects* juftification and life, from the God of all grace, through Chrift; fo it gives the whole *glory* hereof to him.

Thus, as through the blood and righteoufnefs of Chrift, God is declared to be *juft*, in his being *the juftifier of him that believes in Jefus*, Rom. iii. 26: and, in this way, to juftify a finner *freely by his grace*, Tit. iii. 3.: fo faith *receives* this juftifying fentence, proclaimed in the gofpel, and brought home by the Spirit to the foul; and gives all the *glory* of juftification, both as to *forgivenefs* and *acceptance*, to the free *grace* of God, from whence alone it is received.   And therefore the apoftle, in the triumph of faith, challenges all the enemies of God's people, to bring in their accufations, if they have ought to fay againft them, with a *Who fhall lay any thing to the charge of God's elect?*   And nullifies them all, with this one word, *It is God that juftifies*, Rom. viii. 33.   And we are *juftified*, fays he, *freely by his grace*, chap. iii. 24.   As we have *the forgivenefs of fins, through* Chrift's *blood, according to the riches of his grace;* fo, by the fame grace, he *hath made us accepted in the beloved*, Eph. i. 6, 7.—Thus, having fhewn how juftifying faith *acts* towards Chrift, its *immediate*, and God in, and through him, its *ultimate object*, I proceed to the next thing propofed; which was,

3*dly*, To fhew *how*, or in what respects, the justification of a sinner is by *faith†*. When the scripture speaks of being justified by faith; in some places, it is to be taken *objectively*, and not *subjectively*; or, for *Christ*, the *object* of faith, and not for the *grace* of faith, inherent in, and acted by the soul. As, where it is said, Rom. iv. 5. *But to him that worketh not, but believeth on him that justifieth the ungodly, his faith is counted for righteousness.* The word *faith* here, which is said to be counted for righteousness, is not to be understood of the *act* of faith, but of *Christ* the *object* of faith; for the act of faith is not imputed for righteousness, but that which faith lays hold of, *i. e.* the obedience of Christ, which is the object about which the act of faith is conversant. And thus, verse 3. it is said, *Abraham believed God, and it was counted unto him for righ-*

---

† "Faith justifies a sinner in the sight of God,
"not because of those other graces, which do al-
"ways accompany it, or of good works, that are
"the fruits of it, Gal. iii. 11.; nor as if the grace
"of faith, or any act thereof, were imputed to
"him for justification, Rom. iv. 5.; but only as it
"is an instrument, by which he receiveth and ap-
"plieth Christ and his righteousness, John i. 12."
Larger Cat. Q. 73.

teoufnefs *.   Where *Chrift* muft neceffa-rily be underftood by the *it*, that was counted unto him for righteoufnefs.   As is plain from the three laft verfes of the chapter; where it is faid, *Now it was not written for his fake alone, that it was im-puted unto him; but for us alfo, to whom it fhall be imputed, if we believe on him that raifed up Jefus our Lord from the dead; who was delivered for our offences, and raif-ed again for our juftification.*   Since it was the fame *it* that was imputed unto *Abra-ham*, that fhall be imputed unto *us*; hence it appears, that it was not the *act* of *Abra-ham's* faith that was imputed unto *him* for righteoufnefs; becaufe it is not the *act* of his faith that is imputed unto us. But it was the *object* that his faith looked to, the complete obedience of a crucified and rifen *Jefus*, that was imputed unto him for righteoufnefs; and that fhall be im-

---

* It is exceeding obfervable, that it is not faid, Abraham left his country, quitted his idolatry, abandoned his relations, or that he offered his fon, and it was imputed to him for righteoufnefs; but that *Abraham believed God, and* IT *was counted to him for righteoufnefs,* Gen. xv. 6.; which fhews the peculiar dignity and excellency of faith. It is as fingularly fitted and fuited to take hold of Chrift, and his righteoufnefs, as a beggar's hand to receive an alms.

M

puted unto *us*, if we, having the same faith that he had, believe as he did, in Christ for justification, and in God as justifying in, and through him. For, it is *by the obedience of* this *one*, that *Abraham*, and all true *believers*, from the beginning of the world to the end thereof, even all the *many* that shall be saved, are *made righteous*, as chap. v. 19. But, as to be justified by *faith*, in *this sense*, is the same as to be justified by the *righteousness* of Christ, and so respects the *matter* of justification, which I have spoken of under the first general; so I shall pass it here, where I am treating of the *manner* of justification, which, with respect to ourselves, is by *faith*, as *subjectively* and not *objectively* taken: and I shall attend to the manner of justification by *faith*, as *inherent* in, and *acted* by the soul; or shew how, or in what respects, the justification of a sinner is thus by faith. And,

1. It is by *faith*, as it stands opposed to *works*. As saith the apostle, Rom. iii. 28. *Therefore we conclude, that a man is justified by faith, without the deeds of the law.* The justification of a sinner is by faith *alone*, not by faith and works *toge-*

ther; but by faith, *exclusive* of all works, both before and after faith is wrought in the soul. Works done before faith can have no influence into justification; since *by the deeds of the law, no flesh can be justified in* God's *sight.* And works done after believing, are done for no such end, as to make the person righteous before God; nor do they add a whit to his justification in his sight.. So that it is by faith *alone* that a sinner enters into a justified state. Thus, Rom. iv. 5. *To him that worketh not, but* BELIEVETH *on him that justifieth the ungodly, his faith is counted for righteousness.* It is, as if he should say, that is a justified man, that doth no good *works,* nothing at all to obtain it; but *believeth* on *Christ,* for complete pardon, righteousness, and life; and on *God,* as justifying, only in and through him, even the *ungodly.* For, as God in justifying a sinner, through the blood and righteousness of Christ, considers that soul as in itself *ungodly;* so the soul, when it acts faith for justification, sees nothing in itself but *ungodliness:* and under this consideration, of its being a *sinner* and *ungodly,* looks out of itself, un-

to *Chrift*, and unto *God* in him, for all
its juſtification and ſalvation.

Thus the juſtification of a ſinner is by
faith alone; *i. e.* by *faith*, without *works*.
And the apoſtle gives the reaſons of it,
Rom. iv. 16. *Therefore it is of faith, that
it might be by grace, to the end the promiſe
might be ſure to all the ſeed.* It is of *faith,
i. e.* of faith *alone;* (empty-handed faith,
that doth nothing at all for juſtification,
but merely receives it as a free gift) that
it might be by *grace;* that God's free
grace might have the whole glory of juſtification, and all creature boaſting be
for ever excluded.——And it is likewiſe
thus of faith, that the promiſe might be
ſure to all the ſeed. If the promiſe of
juſtification and life, had in the leaſt de-
pended upon the good works of the creature, it could never have been ſure; but
as it ſtands wholly upon grace, abſolute
grace, and is merely received by faith a-
lone, ſo it ſtands *ſure*, inviolably ſure to
all the *ſeed*, to all the heirs of promiſe,
through all time, and unto all eternity.
——Thus the juſtification of a ſinner is
by faith, as it ſtands oppoſed to works,
as to the *manner* of it; or the manner

of the foul's poffeffing Chrift's righteoufnefs.

2. It is by *faith*, as faith is that grace
which is *appointed* of God, to *receive* juftification and life from him. Thus Mark
xvi. 15, 16. *Go ye into all the world, and
preach the gofpel to every creature. He that
believeth, fhall be faved; but he that believeth not, fhall be damned.* And John iii. 36.
*He that believeth on the Son, hath everlaft-
ing life: and he that believeth not the Son,
fhall not fee life; but the wrath of God abideth on him.* And *we,* faith the apoftle,
*have believed in Jefus Chrift, that we might
be juftified by the faith of Chrift;* and this
we did, fays he, as *knowing that a man is
not juftified by the works of the law, but by
the faith of Jefus Chrift;* or, as knowing
that faith is that grace, which God hath
appointed to receive juftification, Gal. ii. 16.
Again,

3. The juftification of a finner is by
faith, as God *imputes* the righteoufnefs of
his Son, and *declares* the imputation thereof, in his *word,* unto every *believer,* for
his complete *juftification.* Thus the righteoufnefs of Chrift is faid to be *unto,* and
*upon all them that believe, without differ*ence,

Rom. iii. 22. *And by him all that believe, are* (declared to be) *juſtified from all things, from which they could not be juſtified by the law of Moſes,* Acts xiii. 39. There is not a believer in the world, that looks to, receives, and depends upon the righteouſneſs of Chriſt alone, for juſtification before God, but God imputes it to him, and juſtifies him, completely therein: For it is unto, and upon all them that believe, without difference. One believer is not *more*; and another *leſs* juſtified; becauſe, though there may be a great deal of difference between the *faith* of one and of another, in reſpect of *degree*; yet all that have faith of the *right kind*, as they *receive* the ſame *righteouſneſs,* the righteouſneſs of Chriſt, for their whole and entire righteouſneſs before God; ſo he *imputes* it to them, as ſuch, and completely juſtifies them all equally, and alike therein. They are all, in this reſpect, *complete in Chriſt;* ſo complete, that nothing can be added to it, to make their juſtification more *full,* Col. ii. 10. And as all believers are *completely* juſtified in Chriſt, by the free-grace, and according to the ſtrict juſtice of God; ſo in him they are *ever-*

lastingly justified. They *stand* immoveably, unchangeably, and eternally in the *grace* of justification, Rom. v. 2. *They are so passed from death to life, that they shall never come into condemnation,* John v. 14. Though in themselves they are sinners, both by nature and practice; yet, as God doth not impute their sins, but the righteousness of his Son to them, for their complete justification; so they have life, everlasting life, in this respect.—But as I shall have occasion to speak more fully of *this,* under the next head; so I shall add no more here.—And thus much shall suffice for the second general, the *manner* of justification, as with respect unto *God,* it is by *imputation;* and with respect to *ourselves,* by *faith.*

S E C T.   III.

Of the T I M E *of Justification.*

Rom. iv. 25. iii. 26. 1 Tim. iii. 16.

*He was delivered for our offences, and raised
    again for our justification.——God is just,
    and the justifier of him that believeth in
    Jesus.——God was justified in the Spirit.*

THE next thing proposed to be
        considered, was, The *time* of justifi-
cation.   As justification is God's act, so
it is to be considered, either as *immanent*,
or *transient*, and timed accordingly.

1. As *immanent*, or an act of God's
will, that always abideth the same in his
divine mind, from eternity to eternity :
and so it was from *everlasting ;* as 2 Cor.
v. 19. *God was in Christ*, (who can tell
how early?   Surely he was in him, by
his eternal counsel, will, and covenant)
*reconciling the world unto himself, not imput-
ing their trespasses unto them.*

2. The act of justification is to be con-

fidered as *tranfient;* or, as it is an act of God that paffeth upon the creature in *time* *. And as fuch, it admits of a two-fold confideration.

(1.) As paffing upon the whole *body* of the *elect* together, and at once, in *Chrift* their *head* and *reprefentative.* And fo the *time* of it was when Chrift, our Surety, made full *payment* of all the debts of his people, and received a full *acquittance,* or a full and open difcharge, in their *name* and *room.* For, he *was delivered for our offences, and raifed again for our juftification,* Rom. iv. 25. As he died, as a *public* perfon, for our fins; fo, as a *public* perfon, he was raifed again for our juftification. When God the Father *raifed* him from the *dead,* he thereby did openly *difcharge* him from all our fins, which before lay upon him; and in *his* difcharge, *we* were difcharged likewife. *He* was difcharged for *us,* and *we* were difcharged in *him,* as he was our great *reprefentative.*

* " Though, from eternity, God *decreed* to
" juftify all the elect; yet they are not *actually*
" juftified, until the Holy Spirit doth, in due time,
" apply Chrift, and his righteoufnefs, unto them,
" 1 Pet. i. 2, 19, 20. Rom. viii. 30. Gal. ii. 16.
" Tit. iii. 4, 5, 6, 7." Conf. chap. xi. § 4.

N

And thus the apostle founds his triumphant challenge, to all the enemies of God's people, to bring ought against them, if they can, Rom. viii. 33, 34. *Who shall lay any thing to the charge of God's elect? It is God that justifieth. Who is he that condemneth? It is Christ that died; yea, rather, that is risen again.* As the *act* of God *justifying*, gives *being* to, and is the *foundation* of our *justification*; so, he first *founds* his triumph *here*, and answers all the charges which might be brought with this, *It is God that justifieth:* and then he proceeds, *It is Christ that died; yea, rather, that is risen again.* So that, by Christ's *death* and *resurrection*, and at the *time* thereof, the whole *body* of the *elect*, as such, had a full *discharge*, a complete *justification*, in *Christ* their *Head.* * But,

* Jesus Christ being once justified himself, Isa. l. 8. 1 Tim. iii. 16.; so all his people are justified in him; and *God is just* in doing so, Rom. iii. 26. Christ died as a public representative for the iniquities of his people, Isa. liii. 11.; and the sacrifice and oblation he offered up was of a sweet-smelling savour unto God, Eph. v. 2. And therefore, Jehovah declares, that he is not only *well-pleased for his righteousness sake,* Isa xlii. 21.; but that he *is near to justify him,* Isa. l. 8.; yea, that he is *justified in the Spirit,*

(2.) Juſtification, as a *tranſient* act, is to be conſidered, as paſſing upon every individual *perſon* of God's choſen; and ſo the *time* of it is, when the ſoul is firſt enabled to *believe in Jeſus*. *For, with the heart man believeth unto righteouſneſs*, Rom. x. 10. *And God is juſt, and the juſtifier of him that believeth in Jeſus*, chap. iii. 26. For, notwithſtanding the *ſecret* ſtate of an elect perſon God-ward, before *believing*, is a ſtate of *peace* and favour, as he has a *ſecret* intereſt in God's juſtifying *act*, and in Chriſt's full *diſcharge*; yet his *open* ſtate, as in *himſelf*, related to old Adam, and the *firſt* covenant, is a ſtate of law-charge, and ſo of wrath and condemnation. He is *of the works of the law*, and as a law-breaker, is under the *curſe*; as *the wrath of God*, in his holy, righteous law, *is revealed from heaven againſt all unrighteouſneſs of men*. He is in the ſame common ſtate with all the children of Adam, of whom it is ſaid, *there is none righteous, no not one*;

---

1 Tim. iii. 16.: and conſequently Chriſt's reſurrection, aſcenſion, ſeſſion at his Father's right-hand, interceſſion for his people, and having all judgment committed to him, is an evidence that all his people are virtually juſtified in him as their head, and ſhall all riſe and reign with him in due time.

and so, a child *of wrath by nature, even as others.* And there is no way, appointed of God, whereby he can pass from this *open* state of *wrath,* and *condemnation by* the law, into an *open* state of *justification* by grace, but by *faith* in Christ : for *he that believeth on the Son, hath everlasting life,* the life of *justification; and he that believeth not the Son, shall not see life, but the wrath of God abideth on him,* John iii. 36. So that, according to the *declaration* of God, in his *word,* by which he will *judge* all men at the last day, no person is in a *justified* state, but he that *believeth* in Jesus. And therefore, the *time* of justification, as applied to a particular *person,* or as God's justifying *act,* passeth upon a sinner, in the declaration of his *word,* and is brought home to the *conscience,* is when the soul *believes ;* or, when being warned of its misery, and acquainted with its remedy, it first flees for refuge, from the wrath to come, to lay hold upon Christ, the hope set before it. And in this sense, *all that believe,* and none but they, *are justified from all things, from which they could not be justified by the law of Moses.*

SECT. IV.

Of the EFFECT of Justification.

ROM. v. 1. iv. 7. 2 COR. v. 14.

Being justified, by faith we have peace with God, through our Lord Jesus Christ.—— Blessed are they whose iniquities are forgiven.——The love of Christ, who died for us, constraineth us to live unto him.

THE next thing I am to consider, is, the *effect* of *justification* with respect to the soul. And this is three-fold, and has respect, 1. Unto the soul's peace. 2. Unto its state. 3. Unto its obedience. To each of these, a little in order. And,

1. The *effect* of *justification*, to a justified soul, is *peace*. As Rom. v. 1. *Therefore, being justified, by faith we have peace with God, through our Lord Jesus Christ.* As Christ, by his death, made peace with God for poor sinners, and as God the Father declared himself to be *the God of peace,* when he *brought again from the dead the Lord Jesus, that great Shepherd of the sheep,*

through the blood of the everlasting covenant;
so this complete and everlasting peace, is
declared, and particularly applied to the
soul, by the blessed Spirit of God, when
it is enabled to believe in Christ for justification. Peace with God was the legacy our departing Lord left with his
people, which was confirmed by the death
of the testator. Thus, John xiv. 27. *Peace,*
says he, *I leave with you; my peace I give
unto you: let not your heart be troubled, neither let it be afraid.* It is as if he should
say, ' My dear disciples, I am just a go-
' ing to leave you, just upon the point of
' finishing all that work which the Father
' gave me to do in the world, for your
' salvation: but when I depart, I will
' leave *peace* with you, *my* peace; that
' peace with God, I shall make by the
' blood of my cross, I *give* unto you. I
' do not give it *partially, conditionally,* and
' *precariously;* I do not give and take, as
' the *world* doth; but my peace I give
' unto you *wholly, absolutely,* and *irrever-*
' *sibly:* therefore, *let not your heart be
' troubled, neither let it be afraid.* Do not
' be troubled that I am going to leave
' you, as to my bodily presence; for, *it*

is expedient for you, that I go away: I go to prepare a place for you. When, as your High-Priest, I have done the work of making peace for you on earth, I have still another work to do for you in heaven; I must carry my peace-making blood, into *the holiest of all,* and sprinkle it before the face of God; and so *reconcile* that holy place, and make room for you to come thither; or thereby, *prepare* those mansions, those abiding places in glory, which are appointed for you. And therefore, *let not your heart be troubled,* since my departure from you is so much for your advantage; *neither let it be afraid,* for as I *made* peace for you, by my death on the cross, so I will *maintain* it for you, by my life on the throne: you need not be afraid that there should be any after-breach between God and you, nor fear the least flaw being made in that peace with God, which I give unto you.' And as this complete and everlasting peace with God, was made by Christ, and is given to his people; so it is applied, by the blessed Spirit, to every believer in particular; as our Lord promised, in the

preceeding verse : *But*, says he, *the Com-forter*, *which is the Holy Ghost, whom the Father will send in my name, he shall teach you all things, and bring all things to your rememberance, whatsoever I have said unto you.* As this verse stands *connected* with the *former*, we may take the scope of our Lord's words thus ; ' Though I am
' going to leave you, *I will not leave you*
' *comfortless* ; *I leave peace with you, I give*
' *peace to you* ; and I will give you the
' *Comforter, whom the Father will send in*
' *my name*, to open this peace to your un-
' derstandings, to apply it to your hearts,
' and bring it to your rememberance, to
' your unspeakable joy, while passing
' through a world of trials.' And ac-
cordingly, when the Spirit of God has revealed the obedience of Christ to the soul, and enabled it to act faith thereon, for justification, he applies the blood of Christ to that soul, by bearing witness to it, of its own particular *interest* in the death of Jesus, and in that *peace* with God, made by his blood ; and hereby gives it *peace* of conscience ; even *true, solid, last-ing peace*, that will abide through *life*, through *death*, at *judgment*, and to *eter-*

nity †. And this peace, is peculiar to a *justified* soul, and a proper *effect* of *justification.*

An *unjustified* soul, indeed, may have some kind of *peace* of conscience, while he works for life, goes about to establish his own righteousness, and quiets his conscience with his own obedience, either present, or resolved on for the future. But this is a *false* peace; conscience is but lulled asleep, and not truly pacified: *as many as are of the works of the law,* that work to make themselves righteous before God, *are under the curse,* Gal. iii. 10.; and therefore must be wicked persons in God's account: and *there is no peace to the wicked, faith my God,* Isa. lvii. 21. *The way of peace they have not known,* Rom. iii. 17. They

---

† Though our author here very strongly affirms the permanency of that peace which a justified person has with God, through the blood of Christ; yet he is not to be understood, as asserting, that the peace of a justified person is never interrupted in a present life, which is very frequently the case, through the prevalancy of the remains of inherent corruption, especially with exercised Christians: he only means, that it is such a peace as the grounds and foundation of it cannot be utterly taken away, being Christ's legacy bequeathed to them; because *he rests in his love,* and *his gifts* and *callings are without repentance.*

O

may cry, *Peace, peace* to themselves; but *sudden destruction* shall come upon them. This miserable, delusive *peace,* cannot stand the test of God's holy law and strict justice, nor abide the storm of his indignation, which shall come down *upon every soul of man that doth evil,* that is in an unrighteous, unjustified state.   The storm of God's wrath, that will meet such a soul at death, will sweep away all this false peace; and nothing but terrors will then surround it.   Conscience, that was once lulled asleep, by a false apprehension of the creature's *goodness,* as if sufficient to make its *peace* with God, will then awake, and, like an enraged lion, gnaw and torment the soul for ever; when, upon the fullest *conviction,* though too late for all *remedy;* it shall see, that nothing could *make* peace with God, for a sinner, nor *give* peace to it, but the *blood and righteousness* of Christ.   And thus the poor soul, being stript *naked* of all its own righteousness and peace, that *hiding-place,* whither it had fled for shelter, that *refuge of lies,* with which it had been deceived, shall stand exposed to all the curses of God's righteous *law,* and the amazing storm of his vindictive wrath, which shall break-forth upon it thereby, and *drown* it in eternal *perdition*. For, the *waters* of God's indignation, *shall overflow the hiding-place of a sinner's own righteousness, and sweep away the refuge of lies*, its false peace, built thereupon, and drive away the naked soul, like an irresistible *torrent*, into the bottomless *gulf* of remediless *torment*, Isa. xxviii. 17, 18.

But he that *believeth* on *Christ*, the *foundation, God has laid in Zion, shall never be confounded*, verse 10. with 1 Pet. ii. 6. He that hath *Christ* for all his righteousness and peace, hath such a *righteousness*, such a *peace*, that shall *abide* for ever. That man, that is *justified* by faith, is a *perfect* man, an *upright* man, in God's account; and concerning him, the Psalmist says, *Mark the perfect man, and behold the upright; for the end of that man is peace*, Psalm xxxvii. 37. And as it is the happiness of the righteous man to *enter into peace*, when he dies, Isa. lvii. 7.; so is it his privilege to have peace while he lives, and that even in the midst of *tribulation;* in the midst of outward *troubles*, he hath inward peace, John xvi. 33.

As for that *false* peace, which the *wicked* have in this world, as it shall perish at last, so it is often broken now, by the flashes of God's *law* in the conscience; which are as many earnests of that approaching storm of his fiery *indignation*, which shall quickly overtake them. And, alas! for these miserable souls, when under pressing afflictions, how are they like the *troubled sea, that cannot rest, whose waters cast up mire and dirt?*——But as for the *righteous* man, he hath *peace*, even in the most trying circumstances; such peace, that the world can neither give, nor take, nor yet can understand. That *peace of God, that keeps his heart and mind, through Christ Jesus, passeth all the understanding* of the natural man, Phil. iv. 7. A justified soul, having his *feet*, his faith, *shod with the preparation of the gospel of peace,* having *peace with God, through Jesus Christ,* is well prepared to pass securely through a *thorny* world. Such an one may safely tread upon all the briers of the wilderness, without fear of danger, since his *shoes* are like *iron and brass,* that will even turn a *thorn,* Eph. vi. 15. Deut. xxxiii. 25.——And, in a word, there is nothing can *hurt* that soul, who, being *justified* by faith, has *peace* with God, neither in this world, nor that to come. So great is the privilege of that *peace*, which is the *effect* of *justification!* Again,

2. The *effect* of *justification*, with respect to the soul, may be considered, with regard to its *state*. And the state of a *justified* soul, is a state of *blessedness*. As soon as ever the soul is enabled to believe in Christ, for justification, and in God, as justifying in and through him, it passes *from death unto life,* John v. 24. It is delivered from the *curse* of the law, and all the *blessings,* both of the law and gospel come upon it. As *Christ has redeemed it from the curse of the law ; so the blessing of Abraham, comes upon it through faith,* Gal. iii. 13, 14. And thus the apostle, speaking of a *justified* state, Rom. iv. 5. calls it a state of *blessedness*, verses 6, 7, 8. *Even as David also describeth the blessedness of the man, unto whom God imputeth righteousness without works, saying, Blessed are they whose iniquities are forgiven, and whose sins are covered. Blessed is the man to whom the Lord will not impute sin:* and verse 9. *Cometh this blessedness then upon the circumcision only,*

or upon the uncircumcision also?—Thus it appears, that a *justified* state, is a state of *blessedness.*

The state of an *unjustified* soul is a state of *wrath;* and such an one is under the *curse* wherever he is, or whatever he does: as Deut. xxviii. 16, 17, 18, 19. The Lord has not only threatened to curse him, by sending upon him *vexation and rebuke*, as verse 20.; but even to *curse his blessings*, his outward enjoyments, as Mal. ii. 2.

But, on the contrary, a *justified* soul is *blessed* in all conditions; his enjoyments are *blessings* to him, and so are his afflictions. *All things are his*, whether comforts or crosses, life or death; *all work together for his good*, and *turn to his salvation*, 1 Cor. iii. 22. Rom. viii. 28. His very *sufferings* are *gifts* of divine favour, Phil. i. 29. And he has reason to *rejoice* even when he *falls into divers temptations;* because of that present and eternal advantage he shall reap thereby, and that peculiar *blessedness*, which attends him therein, James i. 2,—12. A *justified* soul passes on from *blessing* to *blessing*, in every changing providence; for every *change* opens to him a new scene of *blessedness*, to make his enjoyments thereof more full. He is *bleſſed* in proſperity, and *bleſſed* in adverſity; and God over-rules both for his preſent and eternal advantage, and eſpecially his *afflictions*, to increaſe his grace, and prepare him for his crown: ſo that his ſhort-lived *afflictions*, are but *light*; ſince, as God works upon *him* by them, they *work for him, a far more exceeding, and eternal weight of glory*, 2 Cor. iv. 17. A juſtified ſoul has a right to all *bleſſedneſs* now; and ſhall have the full enjoyment of all *bleſſedneſs* hereafter. As he is now delivered from the *curſe*, and fully *bleſt*, even in thoſe very *afflictions* which, in their own nature, are the fruits of the *curſe*; ſo, when God has wrought all that good for him, which was deſigned by them, he ſhall be delivered from the very *being* of theſe grieving things. There ſhall be no grieving briar, nor pricking thorn, no ſin, ſorrow, nor death, to diſturb that reſt, or deſtroy that life of *bleſſedneſs*, which is reſerved for him in the ſtate of glory, in the viſion of God and of the Lamb for ever: as Rev. xxi. 4. *And God ſhall wipe away all tears from their eyes; and there ſhall be no more death, nei-*

ther sorrow, nor crying; neither shall there be any more pain: for the former things are passed away.——And there shall be no more curse; but the throne of God and of the Lamb shall be in it; and his servants shall serve him. And they shall see his face; and his Name shall be in their foreheads. And there shall be no night there; and they need no candle, neither light of the sun; for the Lord God giveth them light: and they shall reign for ever and ever, chap. xxii. 3, 4, 5.

Thus the justified ones, as they are *blest* at all times, shall be *blest* to all eternity. And to acquaint them with their state of blessedness, to comfort their hearts under their present troubles, and in the expectation of their future bliss, the Lord bid the prophet, *say unto the righteous, that it shall be well with him,* Isa. iii. 10. It shall be *well* with him in *life; well* with him at *death; well* with him at *judgment;* and it shall be *well* with him for *ever.*—— It shall be *well* with him in *life;* for, *blessed is the man that trusteth in the* LORD, *and whose hope the* LORD *is,* Jer. xvii. 7, 8.—— It shall be *well* with him at *death;* for, *blessed are the dead that die in the* LORD, Rev. xiv. 13.——It shall be *well* with him at *judgment;* for then he shall be openly pronounced *blessed;* and as such admitted into endless life, or into the inconceivable *blessedness* of *eternal life;* and so it shall be *well* with him for *ever,* Mat. xxv. 34,—46. ——Thus *blessed* is the righteous man! Thus *well* shall it be with him! *But wo unto the wicked; for it shall be ill with him:* his state, in all respects, is just the reverse. How distinguishing then is the favour, how great the privilege of that *blessedness of state,* which is the *effect* of *justification!* * But,

* The privileges and benefits of these persons, who have the Lord to be their righteousness, are very many.—They are not only pardoned, but justified; and their pardon is not only a fruit of mercy, but an act of justice; *God is just in justifying,* Rom. iii. 25, 26.—The justified persons are redeemed from the curse, by Christ's being made a curse for them, Gal. iii. 13.—These who are interested in Christ's righteousness, are delivered from wrath: because he was delivered up to sufferings and death, Rom. viii. 32. he can deliver from wrath, 1 Thess. i. 10.—These who are cloth'd with Christ's righteousness, have a sure and the manent state of justification; *There is no condem tion to them,* Rom. viii. 1.—Justified perso dience a sure and firm standing in the grace and of his God, Rom. v. 2.—These to whom Chri of his righteousness, do also receive the holy of is self-iii. 5, 6.—The prayers of justified pe nd there-ceptable to, and powerful with God fair shew, Spirit encourages them to, and assists t

P

3. In the laſt place, I am to conſider, the *effect* of *juſtification;* as it reſpects the

Prov. xv. 8. *The prayer of the upright is God's delight. The Spirit alſo helpeth our infirmities with groanings which cannot be uttered,* Rom. viii. 26.——All the outward and temporal mercies of juſtified perſons are heightened and ſweetened to them, by the ſpring from whence they flow, and they have a new reliſh. *He delivered me,* ſays David, *becauſe he delighted in me,* Pſalm xviii. 19. *In love to my ſoul,* ſays Hezekiah, *he hath delivered me from the pit of corruption, having caſt all my ſins behind his back,* Iſa. xxxviii. 17.——Juſtified perſons enjoy their temporal favours by God's promiſe, Heb. xi. 9.; and have a ſpiritual right to them by the death of Chriſt, *who is the heir of all things,* Heb. i. 2.——All the afflictions of juſtified perſons *work for their good,* Rom. viii. 28. They are often allayed and mitigated, Ezra ix. 13.; they ſpring from God's care of them, Heb. xii. 6, 7.; they are medicinal to them, Iſa. i. 25.; they are purifying to them, Heb. xii. 10, 11.; they are but ſhort and momentary, 2 Cor. 4, 17.——Death to juſtified perſons, who are clothed with Chriſt's righteouſneſs, is of great advantage; it is theirs, 1 Cor. iii. 22. and to them *great gain,* Phil. i. 21.——Juſtified perſons have a bleſſed and glorious reſurrection ſecured to them in Chriſt their head; for, as they *die in the Lord,* Rom. xiv. 8.; ſo they ſhall be made *alive in Chriſt* 1 Cor. xv. 21, 22. and *raiſed up unto eternal life,* John vi. 54.——In a word, juſtified perſons will ſtand aſſoiled and acquit at the laſt day, becauſe the Judge is their friend, Acts xvii. 31. Iſa. lviii. 11. and the kindly intimation will be iſſued forth, *Come, ye, bleſſed of my Father, inherit the kingdom prepared for you, from the foundation of the world,* Matth. xxv. 34.——O how many are the privileges and inconceivably great the bleſſedneſs of thoſe who are intereſted in the finiſhed righteouſneſs of the adorable Redeemer!

foul's *obedience*.　And as a *juſtified* foul is ſaved from wrath, and has peace with God, as it is redeemed from the curſe, and brought into a ſtate of bleſſedneſs ; ſo it is delivered from *ſervile*, and enabled to yield *filial* obedience.　*It is no more a ſervant, but a Son ;* and obeys its Father, as *an heir of God through Chriſt*, Gal. iv. 7. As a *dear child*, it becomes a *follower of God, and walks in love, as Chriſt alſo has loved it, and given himſelf for it*, Eph. v. 1, 2.　*The love of God ſhed abroad in the heart* of a poor ſinner, *juſtified* by his grace, forms its own image there; and enables the foul to *love* God again, who has *firſt loved* it ; and to ſhew this love, in *keeping his commandments*, Rom. v. 5. 1 John iv. 19. and v. 3. *The love of Chriſt conſtrains it, to live unto him, who died for it, and roſe again for our juſtification*, 2 Cor. v. 14, 15.

An *unjuſtified* foul, as it is under the ſervitude of the law, ſo it is acted by *the ſpirit of bondage ;* and all its obedience to God, ſprings from a ſlaviſh *fear* of his *wrath*, and the main *end* thereof is ſelf-preſervation and deliverance.　And there-fore, notwithſtanding all that *fair ſhew*, which it makes *in the flesh*, all its *legal* obedience which looks so specious in its own and others eyes, God will call it *an empty vine, that brings* forth no *fruit* unto *him*, but all unto *itself*, Hof. x. 1.

But it is quite otherwise with a *justified* soul; such an one is *under grace*, and is acted by *the Spirit of adoption*, which gives him glorious freedom, and abundant liberty to worship and serve God, as his own Father in Christ, from a principle of *love* and *gratitude*, for that great love manifested to him, and that full salvation bestowed upon him; and the main *end* of his obedience is to *glorify* his Father which is in heaven.   And thus the *justified* soul, in his obedience, *brings forth fruit unto God:* as saith the apostle, Rom. vii. 4. *Wherefore, my brethren, ye also are become dead to the law by the body of Christ, that ye should be married unto another, even to him who is raised from the dead, that we should bring forth fruit unto God.*   To *bring forth fruit unto God*, is such a proper *effect* of justification, that it is impossible it should be found in an *unjustified* soul. And therefore the apostle sets forth the deliverance of the *justified* ones, from the

bondage of the *law*, as a covenant of
works, and so from *servile obedience* to it,
by a woman's being *freed from the law of
her husband, when he is dead*; and their
new obligation to gospel-obedience, or to
serve the *law* of God *in the newness of the
Spirit*, by the loosed woman's being *married to another man*, verses 2, 3. As is
evident by his applying, verse 4. what
he had said in the former : *Wherefore my
brethren, ye also are become dead to the law
by the body of Christ*; q. d. You are delivered from the bondage and servitude of
the law, by Christ's fulfilling its requirements for you, and enduring its penalties; by which the law is become *dead*
to *you*, and you to *it*. The *law*, as it is
a covenant of works, that requires doing
for life, and threatens death upon disobedience, has no more obedience to require
of *you*, nor you to yield to *it*, than a *dead*
man has to require of her that was formerly his *wife*; nor than *she* has to yield
to *him* that was formerly her *husband*,
when once the relation is broken. And
then follows, *That ye might be married to
another, even to him who is raised from the
dead, that we might bring forth fruit unto*

God; q. d. You were thus *freed* from the *law,* that you might be *married* unto *Chrift,* as rifen from the dead; that you might be one, everlaftingly one with him, your living head: and fo being completely juftified, in and through him, you might fhare with him, in the power of his end- lefs life; and under the plenitude of his life and bleffednefs, be richly influenced *to bring forth fruit unto God.*

Thus the *juftified* ones are fruitful in *new* obedience: as they *now* regard the *glory* of that God that has juftified them, as the *end* of all their *obedience;* fo they receive his *law,* from their *hufband,* Chrift, as the *rule* of it, and love it as fuch, exceedingly; and thus *ferving the law of God, in the newnefs of the Spirit, and not in the oldnefs of the letter,* or in the grace of the *gofpel,* and not in the terror of the *law,* they *bring forth fruit unto God,* verfe 6.

And, by the way, I look upon this, to be the difcriminating *difference* between a *regenerate* and an *unregenerate* foul. The one obeys as a *flave,* and mainly regards his own *fafety* therein; the other obeys as a *Son,* and the *glory* of God is the chief *end* of his *obedience:* or, the one lives unto *himself*, brings forth fruit unto *himself;* the other lives unto *God,* and brings forth fruit unto *him.* Thus, Rom. xiv. 7. *For none of us liveth to himself,* [*i. e.* none of us who have the life of juſtification beſtowed on us, and the life of ſanctification, or the new-creature life wrought in us] *and no man* [*i. e.* none of us] *dieth to himſelf: But whether we live, we live unto the Lord; or whether we die, we die unto the Lord: whether we live therefore or die, we are the Lord's.* And thus, when he had ſaid of himſelf, and the reſt of the ſaints, whom he ſtiles, *they which live,* [*i. e.* a life of juſtification, and a life of ſanctification, as the effect of Chriſt's death and reſurrection] that *the love of Chriſt conſtrained them, that they ſhould not henceforth live unto themſelves,* in their converſation, *but unto him who died for them, and roſe again,* 2 Cor. v. 14, 15. he adds, verſe 16. *Wherefore henceforth know we no man after the fleſh;* that is, we *approve* of no man, as a *living* man, as a man in *Chriſt,* a *juſtified* and *ſanctified* man; after the *fleſh,* or the *firſt* life: *Yea,* ſays he, *though we have known Chriſt after the fleſh, yet now*

henceforth know we him no more; q. d. We
do not converse with Christ now, as we
once did in the days of his flesh; but as
risen from the dead to a new *life* and glory:
and those who are *risen* with Christ, live
a new *life* unto God, by virtue of his *resurrection;* and these are the men we *know*
and approve of, as living, believing, justified, and sanctified men. As it follows,
verse 17. *Therefore if any man be in Christ,*
[*i. e.* a believer in him, and so a justified
man] *he is a new creature;* [*i. e.* a sanctified man, that lives a new life unto God]
*old things are past away; behold, all things
are become new.* With such an one, *old
dependances* for life, *old enjoyments,* and
old ends in obedience, are past away; and
all things are become *new:* his dependances for life upon Christ, and God in
him, are *new;* his enjoyments of God,
Christ, his people, word, and ordinances,
are *new;* and his life unto God, in obedience, is *new;* or what he never experienced before he was created a new in
Christ Jesus.——Thus it appears, that *new*
obedience, the soul's living unto *God,*
or bringing forth fruit unto *him,* is proper
unto a *justified* and *regenerate* man, and

demonstrative of his *justified* state, and of his being *a new creature*; since all *unjustified unregenerate* souls live unto *themselves*. But, to go on.

As new *obedience* is a proper *effect* of *justification*, and properly belongs to the justified soul, so his privilege, as such, is exceeding great; in that all his works are *accepted*. Those who are washed from their sins in Christ's blood, and clothed with his righteousness, are *made kings and priests unto God, to offer up spiritual sacrifices, acceptable to God by Jesus Christ,* Rev. i. 5, 6. with 1 Pet. ii. 5. *The grace of God, which bringeth salvation,* efficaciously *teacheth* the saved ones, *that denying ungodliness and worldly lusts, they should live soberly, righteously, and godly, in this present world,* Tit. ii. 12. They maintain good works, *for necessary uses, that they may be profitable* unto others, and that they themselves, *may not be unfruitful,* Tit. iii. 8, 14.; and chiefly, that thereby they might *glorify God;* to which they are exhorted, Phil. i. 27. *Only let your conversation be as it becometh the gospel of Christ:* q. d. You saints, have nothing else to do in the world, but to live unto

Q

God, to glorify him, by a conversation becoming the gospel of Christ; which declares your complete justification, and secures your eternal salvation.——Thus the saints are exhorted to *do* good works, and thus they *perform* them.   And all their service is *acceptable* to God, in point of *filial* obedience, though not in point of *justifying* righteousness.   As for this end, they do not perform good works; so, blessed be God, for this end they do not need them.   No; they have a complete justifying righteousness, wrought out by Christ, a glorious robe, which they themselves have no hand in, nor put the least finger to prepare; and are so completely justified in Christ, that nothing can be added to it, to make their justification more *full*.   But though none of their good works go to the stock of their *justification*; yet all of them go to the treasure of their filial *obedience;* and are *acceptable* to God, by Jesus Christ, and shall be openly *rewarded* at his next appearing.   And both the *acceptableness* of the saints service to God, and the *advantage* they themselves shall reap thereby, are proposed to them, as encouragements to be abundant and conftant in the performance of good works.

Thus, Heb. xiii. 15, 16. *By him there-fore let us offer the facrifice of praife to God continually; that is, the fruit of our lips, giving thanks to his name. But to do good, and to communicate forget not, for with fuch facrifices God is well-pleafed.*——*And he that in thefe things ferveth Chrift, is acceptable to God,* Rom. xiv. 18.; that is, in point of *obedience.* And therefore the apoftle, for himfelf, and in the name of the reft of the apoftles, *befeecheth* the faints, the brethren, whofe perfons were already *made accepted in the Beloved,* in point of *righteoufnefs* before God, and *exhorts them by the Lord Jefus, that as* they had *re-ceived of* them *how they ought to walk, and to pleafe God,* i. e. in point of obedience, fo they *would abound more and more,* 1 Theff. iv. 1.: q. d. Since the good works, the filial *obiedience* of you *juftified* ones, are fo *acceptable* by Chrift unto God your Father; fee that you labour to be abun-dant and conftant therein. And as the *acceptablenefs* of the faints fervice to God, is propofed as an encouragement to their filial obedience; fo likewife the *advan-*

tage which they themfelves fhall reap thereby.

As, 1 Cor. xv. 58, 59. *Wherefore, my beloved brethren, be ftedfaft, unmoveable, always abounding in the work of the Lord; forafmuch as ye know that your labour is not in vain in the Lord.* No; thofe whofe *perfons* are accepted in Chrift, and their *obedience* accepted through him, fhall have all their good works *rewarded,* by the fame *grace,* that enabled them to the performance thereof. Thefe fhall find, that *in keeping* God's *commandments there is great reward,* Pfalm xix. 11.

The fervice of God carries its own reward in it now; that peace of confcience, that joy in the Holy Ghoft, that life of the divine favour, that honour God puts upon his people, in his appearances for them, and thofe fore-taftes of glory, they are favoured with, while walking with him, in the *obedience* of children, are a *reward* fo great, that none can either know or enjoy, but thofe who are brought into *the glorious liberty of the fons of God.* But, O the exceeding greatnefs of that *reward,* that is referved for them in the day of Chrift! As all their fervices are now accepted; fo they fhall then appear to be fo, by their being openly *rewarded*.

There is none of their fervice, though fo fmall as the giving *of a cup of cold water to a difciple, in the name of a difciple, that fhall in any wife lofe its reward*, Mat. x. 41, 42. All their obedience, both in heart and life, fhall *be found unto praife, honour, and glory, at the appearing of Jefus Chrift*, 1 Pet. i. 7. *And all the churches fhall know*, faith our Lord, *that I am he that fearcheth the reins and hearts; and I will give unto every one of you according to your works*, Rev. ii. 23. *To him that overcometh*, fays he, *will I grant to fit with me in my throne, as I alfo overcame, and am fet down with my Father in his throne*, chap. iii. 21. *And behold, I come quickly, and my reward is with me; to give every man according as his works fhall be*, chap. xxii. 12.

And, in fhort, the chief defign of our Lord, in what he ordered his fervant John, to write to the Afiatick churches, where he commends their obedience, and reproves what was wanted therein, was, to ftir them up to a *zealous* performance of good *works ;* and the *motive* he uſed hereto was, that the *crown* of glory which he would give unto them, as the *reward* of their obedience, at his appearing and kingdom; which, in greatneſs, ſhould be proportioned, according to the *degree* of their *ſervices* done for him in the preſent ſtate.

He acquaints them with thoſe ſpecial *favours,* thoſe particular *honours* which he had in reſerve for thoſe of his *ſervants,* who had moſt diſtinguiſhed themſelves in his *ſervice.* And hence will ariſe all thoſe different degrees of *glory,* in which the ſaints ſhall ſhine, *at the reſurrection of the juſt.* They will all be bright and glorious, and *ſhine as the ſtars for ever and ever ;* and yet *as one ſtar differeth from another ſtar in glory, ſo ſhall it be in the reſurrection of the dead,* 1 Cor. xv. 41, 42. As the *ſtars* now ſhine with different *glories,* ſo ſhall the *ſaints* then: for thoſe who have *done* and *ſuffered* moſt for Chriſt, in this life, ſhall have an higher ſphere of *glory,* and ſhine with a ſuperior *brightneſs* in the life to come.

And while the ſaints, with Moſes, have *reſpect unto this recompence of the reward,* their *filial* obedience is quickened thereby. *Wherefore we labour*, says the apostle, *that whether present or absent we may be accepted of him*, 2 Cor. v. 9. They did not labour to be *accepted*, in point of *righteousness* before God; for so they already had an acceptance in Christ so full, that none of their labours could add any thing to it. But they laboured to be *accepted*, with regard to their *obedience*; or, they laboured in the whole of their conversation to *walk worthy of the Lord unto all pleasing*; i. e. to walk worthy of their high *relation* to him, those great *favours* they enjoyed from him, and that eternal *interest* they had in him, unto all *pleasing*; or, unto all *acceptable* obedience here, and to the open *acceptation* thereof, in the day of Christ.

And the earnestness of their souls herein, the apostle sets forth by *running of a race, for a prize, or crown*, 1 Cor. ix. 24, 25. *Know ye not that they which run in a race, run all, but one obtaineth the prize? So run that ye may obtain. And every man that striveth for the mastery, is temperate in all things: now they do it to obtain a corruptible crown, but we an incorruptible.*

And as the *prize*, fore-viewed, quickens the faints in the *race*; so that *crown of righteoufnefs* they shall receive, when their *courfe is finished*, will be a rich and abundant *reward* of all their labours; in which the glory of God's free grace, and the greatnefs of its provifion, for thefe favourites of heaven, shall for ever shine forth. *Then, they which feared the Lord, that fpeak often one to another,* (whofe thoughts, words, and works for God, he gracioufly regarded, and accepted here) shall be openly *rewarded,* and appear to be *his,* by that bright glory he will put upon them, in the day when he *makes up his jewels.* When the *wicked,* to their utmoft *horror,* and everlafting *confufion, shall return and difcern between the righteous and the wicked, between him that ferveth God, and him that ferveth him not,* Mal. iii. 16, 17, 18.——It being the peculiar privilege of the *juftified* ones, to have all their *obedience,* thus *accepted* and *rewarded:* fo that, though the good *works* of the faints do not go to the ftock of their juftifying *righteoufnefs;* yet as they go to the treafure of their filial *obedience,* which is fo *acceptable* to God, and shall be fo *rewarded* by him, there is encouragement enough for them, to have an univerfal and conftant regard unto all God's *commandments.* —*The effect of righteoufnefs fhall be peace, quietnefs, and affurance for ever,* Ifaiah xxxii. 17.

Thus I have confidered, the doctrine of *juftification,* or the juftification of a finner in the fight of God,—in the *matter* of it, *i. e.* the complete *obedience* of Jefus Chrift, exclufive of all the *works* of the creature;—in the *manner* of it, as with refpect unto God, it is by *imputation,* and with refpect to ourfelves, by *faith;*—in the *time* of it, as it refpects the whole *body* of the *elect,* and every individual *perfon* of God's *chofen;*—and in the *effects* of it, with refpect to the *foul,* as it regards its *peace,* its *flate,* and its *obedience.*——And what I have briefly faid hereon, I take to be the *fcripture* doctrine of *juftification;* and that which our *proteftant* reformers earneftly *contended* for, at the time of their firft *reformation* from *popery,* as the main *bafis* on which it was founded. And this doctrine of juftification, by the free-grace of God, through the righteoufnefs of Chrift, received by faith alone, was of

R

such great account with Luther, that he said of it, ' The church either stood or ' fell, as this was maintained or re-' jected.'

* * *

SECT. V.

An OBJECTION, urged against the preceding Scripture-Doctrine of *Justification*, answered.

JAMES ii. 21.

Was not Abraham our father justified by works, when he had offered his son Isaac upon the altar?

BUT against what has been said, some may object, thus;

Object. ' The justification of a sinner is ' not by *faith* alone, but by *works* also, ' as is plainly implied in that *text*, 1 John ' iii. 7. *He that doth righteousness, is righ-* ' *teous, even as he is righteous.* And fully ' exprest, James ii. 24. *Ye see then how*

' *that by works a man is juſtified, and not*
' *by faith only.*' To which I anſwer,

Anſw. That the truth laid down, of
juſtification by faith alone, is not in the
leaſt ſhaken by this *objection*, founded upon
theſe *texts*, we ſhall now evince.

As to the firſt, *He that doth righteouſneſs, is righteous :* it is not to be under-
ſtood, as if that perſon was righteous, by
his *doing* of righteouſneſs ; but that by
his *doing* of righteouſneſs, it was manifeſted that he was a *righteous* perſon. And
therefore the apoſtle begins the verſe, with
a *let no man deceive you ;* q. d. - Do not
take every man for a *righteous* man, a
juſtified man in the ſight of God, that
may pretend thereto ; but look into his
converſation, and ſee whether his *faith* in
Chriſt for *juſtification*, produceth fruits of
righteouſneſs in his life : if not, you may
depend upon it, that he is not a righteous
man ; if he is an unrighteous man, in the
general courſe of his *converſation*, he is
certainly ſuch an one, that is not righteous by *imputation :* for, *he that doth
righteouſneſs, is righteous ;* i. e. he is *ſo*
to begin with, before his doing of righteouſneſs ; even *perfectly* ſo, *as He*, [*i. e.*

Chrift] *is righteous;* the perfect obedience
of Jefus Chrift, being imputed to him,
for his complete juftification before God.
And whoever is thus righteous by *imputation,* is likewife righteous by *impartation,*
as having a principle of righteoufnefs *im-
parted* to him, and *inherent* in him; and
from thence he is righteous in his *converfation.* And by his thus doing of righteoufnefs, in his converfation before *men,*
it may be fully *known,* that he is fuch an
one, that is under the imputed righteoufnefs of Chrift, for his juftification before
God: and therefore, verfe 10. he fays,
*In this the children of God are manifeft, and
the children of the devil: whofoever doth not
righteoufnefs, is not of God, neither he that
loveth not his brother.* He doth not fay,
he that doth not righteoufnefs, is not of
God, *becaufe* he doth it not, as if the not
doing of it, made him to be not of God;
but by his not doing of righteoufnefs, it
is *manifeft,* or made to appear, that he is
not of God. And thus we are to underftand him, verfe 7. where, by *he that
doth righteoufnefs, is righteous,* we are to
apprehend, that a righteous perfon's doing
of righteoufnefs, is only *evidential,* and

not *constitutive*, of him as such. And so this *text*, implies no contradiction against the doctrine of a sinner's justification before God, by *faith* alone. And,

As to the other *text*, that *by works a man is justified, and not by faith only*: though justification by *works* be fully exprest, yet it is another *kind* of justification that is here spoken of, than *that*, by *faith*, which I have asserted; and so, is no contradiction to it: the apostle Paul saith, Rom. iii. 28. *That by faith a man is justified, and not by the deeds of the law;* and the apostle James here, *that by works a man is justified, and not by faith only.* And though there is a seeming contradiction between them in *terms*; yet there is really none in *sense*. Because the apostle Paul speaks of the *justification* of a sinner before God, or his real state of justification, God-ward, which is by faith alone; and the apostle James of the *apparency* of the *truth* of his faith, and *so* of his justified state before God, by his good *works* before men; by which only it can be *known* to them. So that while one asserts *real* justification before God, to be by *faith* alone; and the other, *apparent* justification

before *men*, to be by good *works*, flowing
from faith ; there is no contradiction, but
a glorious harmony between them.   Inafmuch as that *faith*, by which a finner
is juftified before God, will certainly be
productive of good *works ;* which *evidence*
a ftate of *juftification* before men.

. And that the apoftle Paul did fpeak
of a ftate of real juftification before *God*,
when he afferts it to be by *faith*, without
the deeds of the law, is evident, verfe 20.
where he likewife excludes the deeds of
the law, from having any hand in the
juftification of a finner ; and what kind
of juftification he intends, he expreffeth
by thofe words, *in his fight. Therefore
by the deeds of the law there fhall no flefh
be juftified* IN HIS SIGHT ; or, before
God.

. And as for the apoftle James, it is e-
vident, that he fpake of a ftate of juftification before *men*, or an apparent ftate of
juftification before them, when he afferts
it to be by *works*, and not by faith only:
for, verfe 18. he fays, *Yea, a man may
fay, thou haft faith, and I have works :*
To which he replies, *Shew me thy faith*
WITHOUT *thy works, and I will fhew thee*

my faith BY *my works.* As he profeffeth to *fhew* his *faith,* and fo his *juftification* by his *works,* it is plain, that he intends an apparent, or manifeftative juftification before *men,* when he afferts it to be by *works.* And this will further appear, by the inftance he gives of Abraham's juftification hereby, verfes 21, 22. *Was not Abraham our Father juftified by works, when he had offered Ifaac his Son upon the altar? Seeft thou how faith wrought with his works, and by works was faith made perfect?* By the word *made* here, we are to underftand, *manifefted;* i. e. that by his works, his faith was manifefted to be *perfect;* or of that perfect *kind,* to which the promife of juftification is annexed. For the word *made* in this *text,* is to be underftood juft in the fame fenfe as it is, 2 Cor. xii. 9. *My ftrength is made perfect in weaknefs.* As from *this* text, we are not to think that the weaknefs of the creature can add any *perfection* to the almighty *power* of God in *itfelf,* but only in its *manifeftation,* as thereby the *power* of God appears to be *perfect,* or ftands forth to be *beheld* in its own *almightinefs;* fo, neither from the *other* are we to apprehend, that

Abraham's works did add any *perfection*
to his *faith* in *itself*, but only in its *mani-
festation*; as thereby his *faith* appeared to
be *perfect*, or stood forth to be *beheld* by
men, in its own *perfection*; as being of
that very *kind* which receives *justification*
from God, and accompanies the *salvation*
of the foul: as it follows, verse 23. *And
the scripture was fulfilled which faith,
Abraham believed God, and it was imputed
unto him for righteousness; and he was called the friend of God.*   In the former part
of this verse, Abraham's justification before *God*, is plainly afferted to be by *faith*,
he believed God, and IT [*i. e.* the obedience
of Christ, which his faith saw in the pro-
mise] *was imputed unto him for righteousness.*
And then, in the latter part of the verse,
his justification before *men* is plainly implied to be by *works*; in as much as his
faith, fo worked by love, in obedience to
God's commands, that *he was called the
friend of God.*   And thus the apostle James,
when he speaks of Abraham's justification
before *God*, afferts it to be by *faith*, as
much as Paul; and when he speaks of it
by *works*, he intends that only which he
had before *men*.   And in this fenfe, the

apostle Paul asserts justification by *works*, as much as James, Rom. iv. 2. *For, if Abraham was justified by works, he hath whereof to glory, but not before God.* This *if* here is not to be taken for an *interrogation*, a question, whether he was or not; but for a *concession*, a grant that he was. And therefore, follows, *he hath whereof to glory; but* (where?) *not before God.* No, no, says the apostle; had he been justified by *works*, before *God*, he would have had whereof to *glory* before *God;* but since his justification by *works*, extended only to *men*, his *glorying* was *there* limited; and all *boasting*, both from *him*, and his *seed*, is for ever *excluded, by the law of faith,* chap. iii. 27.: that is, by the *doctrine* of faith, the *gospel;* which reveals the *obedience* of Christ to be the only justifying *righteousness* of a sinner before God, as it is *imputed* to him, of the freest *grace*, and *received* by *faith* alone. *

* Besides what has been so pertinently advanced above, in answer to the objection urged against the free justification of guilty sinners, by the imputation of the complete obedience and finished righteousness of the divine Redeemer, received by faith, exclusive of all works done by the creature, an attention to the following particulars will throw some farther light thereon, and fully evince, that there is no con-

Thus I have endeavoured to answer the objection made against this doctrine,

tradiction between the apostle Paul in affirming, *That God imputeth righteousness without works,* &c. Rom. iv. 5, 6.; and the apostle James, saying, *Ye see then, how that by works a man is justified, and not by faith only,* James ii. 24.

In order to illustrate this we must carefully distinguish between the several sorts of persons that Paul and James had to do with.—Paul's discourse is bent against proud self-righteous *justiciaries,* who thought to build up a righteousness of their own, by which they designed both to adorn themselves in the eye of God's holiness, and to secure themselves from the sword of his justice: and therefore Paul teacheth, that no righteousness of man can weigh in God's balance, or is pleadable at the bar of justice. *We are all as an unclean thing, and our righteousness is but as filthy rags. By the deeds of the law shall no flesh living be justified,* Rom. iii. 20, 21. But James hath to do with boasting and self-deceiving *hypocrites,* who pretend to faith, but it is a barren, idle, dead faith. They say they had faith, but they had no works, James ii. 14.; they could not shew, or evidence their faith, because they had no works: and therefore his design was, to shame, confound, and silence these hypocrites, and to demonstrate, that they had no true faith at all, but did grasp a lye, and hug an idol of their own, instead of true faith.—Paul treats of faith, as it respects *Christ's righteousness,* and as it builds and is acted only on this before God. But James speaks of faith, as it is to come forth, and to be demonstrated before *men* —The justification that James speaks of is not a justification of the *person,* but of the *faith* of Abraham, of his sincerity and integrity, Gen. xx. 12. But the justification that Paul treats of, is the jus-

I before laid down, by opening the *texts* on which it was founded; and I have

tification of the *ungodly perfon*, by the imputation of Chrift's righteoufnefs, Rom. iv. 5, 6.—Paul treats of the *caufes* of juftification, he fearches after the fprings of it, *viz.* Chrift's righteoufnefs, and faith as receiving it: but James fpeaks of the *effects* of juftification. A man whofe perfon is juftified before God, will certainly juftify his faith and fincerity before men, by works of righteoufnefs.—Paul fpeaks of the juftification of a *finner;* James treats of the approbation of a *believer.* Paul difcourfes of the *righteoufnefs* that muft juftify, *viz.* the righteoufnefs of Chrift; James treats of the *faith* that muft evidence a perfon juftified, of what kind it muft be, *viz.* not an idle, lazy, but an operative faith. Paul fpeaks of juftification before *God*, Rom. iii. 20, 21.; James treats of juftification before *men*, James ii. 18. *Shew me thy faith;* that is, prove it, if thou canft, to be a right faith, if it bring not forth good works.

Moreover, that the apoftle James doth not fpeak of a *proper* juftification of the perfon of a man before God, by works, might be made evident by feveral arguments.—The proper juftification of a man is from *fins* that he hath been guilty of; not for *works of righteoufnefs* which he hath wrought: good works are not fhewed before God's tribunal; but iniquities are *covered*, Pfalm xxxii. 1, 2.—Nothing will properly juftify a perfon, but what is *commenfurate* to the divine law, and will *fatisfy* the juftice of God: but no obedience of ours can do this; nothing but the finifhed righteoufnefs of Chrift: therefore we cannot be juftified by our works; the man that is juftified, is μὴ ἐργαζόμενος, *he that worketh not*, Rom. iv. 5.—Nothing will properly juftify us, but what juftified *Jefus Chrift;* he could not been the larger herein, in order to set *them*, and the *truth*, in a clear light.

be juftified, except he had fulfilled the precept of the law, and endured the curfe alfo in his death : therefore we cannot be juftified by our works; if we could, then would Chrift have died in vain.——In a proper juftification, we are juftified *before God,* Rom. iii. 20, 21. But our own good works cannot be imputed unto us for a righteoufnefs before God, becaufe he fees fo many faults, blemifhes, and defects in them.——Our beft works need a *pardon;* and therefore cannot be our righteoufnefs to juftify us : that which needs forgivenefs, and really deferves punifhment, can never earn a reward, and be accepted for a juftifying righteoufnefs.——If we could be juftified by our good works, we fhould juftify *ourfelves;* but it is *God's act,* and not ours to juftify, Rom. viii. 33. *It is God that juftifeth.*——In true juftification, we *receive* a righteoufnefs and an atonement, Rom. v. 11, 17. But our works cannot make an atonement for us, or be a righteoufnefs to us.

SECT. VI.

The INSUFFICIENCY of legal obedience to the Justification of a Sinner.

ROM. iii. 20.

By the deeds of the law, there shall no flesh be justified in his sight.

AND now, to shew the *impossibility* of a sinner's being *justified* before God, by the *works* of the law, or by his own obedience to the law, I shall take a little notice, what it is that God, by his *law*, requires of man; and also, for what *end* the law was given. And,

First, God, by his *law*, requires of every man *perfect obedience;* which is his duty to perform, although he cannot do it. As all men are creatures of God's *making*, and were all at once made representatively, in their natural head Adam; so in him, as their covenant head, they were creatures of God's *governing;* when he gave him the fundamental *law* of nature, commanding him to eat of the trees of the garden, with a particular prohibition of the tree of knowledge of good and evil, Gen. ii. 16, 17. *And the* LORD *God commanded the man, saying, Of every tree of the garden thou mayst freely eat: But of the tree of knowledge of good and evil, thou shalt not eat of it; for in the day thou eatest thereof, thou shalt surely die.* And it was meet that God should govern the creature he had made both for his own *glory,* and the creature's *good:* for, as God's manifestative *glory* was concerned in his creature's obedience; so it was the *happiness* of the creature to serve its Creator, and in this way to enjoy him. God is so great, so good, and so glorious a Being, that it is the happiness of the angels in heaven to be subject to his commands; and so it was of man in paradise, to be subject to this law given him: in which, though the threatening of dead, upon his disobedience, be only *expressed;* yet the promise of life, or the continuation of that blissful state he was then in possession of, for himself and his seed, upon his o-

bedience, was *implied.*—And this original
law did summarily contain all the *ten
words* given at *mount Sinai,* or the sub-
stance of the moral *law,* delivered in the
ten commandments, by the Lord's audible
voice from heaven; and wrote by him,
in the *two tables of stone,* when he gave
his *law,* in this peculiar manner unto
Israel. And when this moral *law,* in
the original *form* of it, was first given to
Adam, and in him to all *mankind,* his
heart was perfectly conformed thereto;
and he, and so they in him, had *power*
to have kept it; and it would have been
his, and their *happiness,* so to have
done.

But he, being a *mutable* creature, and
left to the freedom of his own *will,* soon
hearkened to the temptations of *Satan,*
cast off his loyalty to his *Maker* and Sove-
reign *Lord,* and yielded subjection to the
prince of darkness, in obeying his *dictates,*
and eating of the forbidden *fruit.* In
doing which, he for *himself,* and his whole
posterity, broke the whole *law* at once.
From whence, the *penalty,* or threatening,
became righteously due to him and them,
as the just reward of his *disobedience,* where-

by *many were made sinners : and so death passed upon all men in him, in whom all had sinned*, Rom. v. 12, 19.

And as soon as Adam had sinned, and we in him, there was thenceforth no *life* to be had for a fallen creature, by its own *obedience* to the law: because the *law* being once *broken*, Adam and every one of his *race*, were looked upon in the eye of the law, as *transgressors ;* and therefore the righteous *law*, could do nothing to *justify* a *sinner;* it became *weak*, in this regard, through our *flesh*, or corrupt nature, Rom. viii. 3: But all the power it had, considered as *broken*, was to thunder out curse and wrath, against every soul of man that had done evil.

And besides the *guilt* of the first transgression, on which account Adam, and all his *posterity*, were at once laid under the curse; from which they could never deliver themselves, and so no life for them by a broken *law*, which bound them over to punishment; besides this, I say, there was an universal *pollution* of nature, that overspread the soul of Adam, the *curse* taking hold upon him in the very *instant* of his disobedience. The threa-

tening was, *In the day thou eatest thereof,
thou shalt surely die;* or, *in dying thou shalt
die.* In which was contained *death* spiritual, temporal, and eternal, as the just
wages of sin. And the *first* of these was
instantly executed upon him: in that very
day, hour, and moment, in which he
sinned, he *died*, in his soul, or spirit, with
regard to that life of holiness, and perfect
conformity to the law, which before he
was possessed of: and thereby he lost all
his *power* to fulfil the law, or to yield
such an obedience as the holy law of God
requires, or can accept. The law *requires*
perfect obedience, and can *accept* of no
less; and Adam having lost all his moral
rectitude, he was utterly incapable to *fulfil*
the law. And as it was with Adam in
this regard, on account of his *first* sin, so
it is with every one of his *descendants*, that
proceed from him by ordinary generation:
as they became *guilty* in *his* first transgression, so coming into the world, in *union*
to him, as their covenant-head, standing
together with him, under the same broken
law, they become *filthy* likewise; the
contagion of sin overspreads the whole
soul, as soon as ever it informs the body.

T

And thus every child of Adam, being *shapen in iniquity, and conceived in sin,* comes forth into this world a *sinner,* with a defiled nature, a *carnal mind,* or corrupt soul, *which is not subject to the law of God, neither indeed can be,* Psalm li. 5. Rom. viii. 7.

And that *infants* are born *sinners,* appears from Rom. v. 14.; where the apostle, proving that sin was in the world, before the giving of the law at *mount Sinai,* in that *death reigned from Adam to Moses,* gives the *death* of *infants* as an instance of their being *sinners. Nevertheless,* says he, *death reigned from Adam to Moses, even over them that had not sinned after the similitude of Adam's transgression:* that is, over *infants,* who were not capable of sinning *actually,* as Adam did; but they being *guilty* in him, and *filthy* from him, the law of God finds them *sinners,* and so *death, the wages of sin,* seizes upon them.

Thus we are sinners by *nature,* before we are so by *practice:* and *none can bring a clean thing out of an unclean ; no not one,* Job xiv. 4. There can be no pure *obedience* yielded to God's holy law, such as it requires, by *filthy, abominable man.* And as *Adam,* upon his first sin, became *guilty,* and *we* in him; and as *he* instantly thereupon became *filthy,* and *we* as soon as we have a being; so there can be no *life* for a fallen creature, by the works of the law. For, *first,* he has already *broken* the law, and so is under the *curse.* And, *secondly,* he has lost his *power* to obey it; and so cannot obtain the *blessing.* And therefore, when Adam had sinned, *The* LORD *God drove out the man from the garden of Eden, and placed cherubims and a flaming sword, that turned every way to keep the way of the tree of life,* Gen. iii. 24. This did signify to him, and to all his posterity, that now he had broken the law, there was no life for them by their own obedience; or that it was impossible that fallen man, should have life by his obedience to the law, as Adam was to have had in *Paradise;* and that whoever should attempt it that way, must be inevitably destroyed by the *flaming-sword* of God's justice, *which turned every way,* towards every one of the commandments, which man had broken, to keep the sinner from life by the law. And therefore, the apoftle fays, That as many as in vain, attempt to obtain life by the law, are under the *curfe*, Gal. iii. 10. *For as many as are of the works of the law, are under the curfe: for it is written, Curfed is every one that continueth not in all things written in the book of the law, to do them.*

Thus there is no life for a fallen creature by the works of the law; becaufe he has loft his *power* to yield fuch an obedience as the law requires. For, the eternal law of God *requires* the fame perfect, perpetual obedience, now man is *fallen*, and has loft his *ftrength*, as it did when he was *upright*, and had *power* to perform it, and that *righteoufly* too. Becaufe, when the law was firft given to Adam, and in him to all *mankind*, he had *power* to have kept it; and though man, by fin, has loft his power to *obey*, yet God has not loft his power to *command*. And therefore, every man that cometh into this world, notwithftanding his being born a *finner*, and previoufly under the *curfe*, is bound to yield a perfect *obedience* to God's holy law, in thought, word, and deed; in heart, lip, and life, from his birth, to his death, without the leaft failure, or wry step; and upon default hereof, he righteously falls under the *condemnation* of the law, and the fiery indignation of a sin-revenging God; which must be born, either by *himself* or his *Surety*, as, blessed be God, it hath been by the *Surety, Christ*, for all that shall be *saved.* And as for those that *perish*, they must bear the weight of their own *sins*, and of God's inexpressible *wrath*, breaking forth upon them, through the curses of a broken law, in the torments of hell for ever.

And this shews the great misery, and cruel bondage we are in by nature, by reason of *sin*, as being under the *law*, which is the *ministration* of *death*, 2 Cor. iii. 7. It *commands* duty, and that *righteously*, but can give no *strength*; and this was shadowed forth by the *bondage* the children of *Israel* were in, in *Egypt*, under *Pharaoh*, and his cruel *task-masters;* who commanded the *full tale of brick, and yet afforded no straw.* And it was an *unrighteous* thing in *them*, thus to command the *Israelites*, and then to *beat* them for the non-performance of that, which they never had *ability* to do; yet, as was said, it is a *righteous* thing with God, according to his law, to command perfect *obedience* of *fallen* man, and to curse him to *death*, upon default hereof; becaufe he once had power to have yielded it, and by his own fin deprived himfelf hereof. But however righteous it is, (as thofe that perifh fhall one day own, *When every mouth fhall be ftoped, and all the world become guilty before God*, Rom. iii. 19.) yet the mifery of man by reafon hereof, is exceeding great.   And,

Secondly, To *fhew* this, *viz*. the mifery of man, by fin, as being under the exacting and condemning law, and fo the need he had of a Saviour, was one great end of the *giving* of the *law* at *mount Sinai*. For, *until the law*, fays the apoftle, *Sin was in the world; but fin is not* IMPUTED *when there is no law*, Rom. v. 13.   How is that?   Why, it is not to be underftood, as if *God* did not *impute* it; for that *he* did, is evident, in that he inflicted the punifhment thereof, the wages due to it, *death: for death reigned from Adam to Mofes*, as in the next verfe.   But the meaning is, that during that tract of time, from Adam to Mofes, the confciences of men were grown in a great measure *secure,* and not having that just sense they ought to have had of the law's severity, (as it was given out to Adam, and to *them* in him) they did not do their office, in condemning for sin. When they did evil, they did not *impute sin* unto *themselves;* or, at least, not in such a manner as they ought, or was agreeable to the strictness of the holy law; and therefore it amounted to little more, nay, no more, in the phrase of the Holy Ghost, than a *non-imputation* of it. And therefore God would have his law come forth in a new edition, with the tremenduous Majesty, and amazing terror of a GOD, *glorious in* HOLINESS; *when he came down on mount Sinai, in flaming fire, with thunders, and lightenings, and a great earthquake; and the voice of a trumpet, founding exceeding loud,* to summons the people to hear the voice of their Creator, GOD, in his holy law, which he summed up, and gave in ten words, or the *ten commandments,* Exod. xix. 16, *&c.* and xx. 1, *&c.* Whereupon *the people removed, and stood afar off;* as struck with the amazing *purity* of God's *nature,* displayed in his holy *law;* while he appeared as *a confuming fire*, to fhew his juft vengeance againft all *law*-breakers: and they being *guilty*, and *felf*-condemned, began to fee their need of a *Mediator*; and faid to Mofes, (the *typical* one) *Speak thou with us, and we will hear ; but let not God fpeak with us, left we die*, verfes 18, 19.——Thus *the law entered that the offence might abound; that fin by the commandment might become exceeding finful*; or appear to be finful fin indeed, Rom. v. 20. and vii. 13.

The *end* of the *law*'s being *given* on *mount Sinai*, to *fallen* man, was not that he fhould obey it for *life ;* but that, by the apparent ftraightnefs of the *rule*, the crookednefs of his *ways* might be *manifeft ;* and that by the ftrict purity of this holy *law*, now drawn out in all its beautiful lineaments, the defilement of man's *nature*, and the odioufnefs of his *features*, in his difconformity thereto, might appear: and that by this *law*, in the hand of the Spirit, which was at firft *ordained unto life*, but now by *fin*, become *the miniftration of death*, the finner might be *killed*, as to all hopes of life therefrom, *the offence thereby abounding in his fight unto death ;* that so by *this* he might be prepared to receive the *free gift* of life in Christ, and the superabounding *grace* of God, *reigning through righteousness, unto eternal life* by him.

Again, the *Sinai* law was *given*, that *Christ* might be made *under* it, to fulfil its *requirements*, and suffer its *penalties* for his people; to make them *righteous* by *his obedience* to it, or the *active* obedience of his *life*, and to redeem them from the curse of it by his *passive* obedience, or his meritorious *death*. And that thus *fulfilling* it, he might become *the end of* it *for righteousness* unto them, and for ever deliver them from it, as it is a covenant of works; that so from *him*, their Saviour-King, they might receive this royal *law*, as a *rule* of life, to square their obedience by; which is designed to glorify God, and not to obtain salvation from: and thus in love, *Serve it, in the newness of the Spirit, and not in the oldness of the letter*, Rom. v. 19. Gal. iii. 13. with chap. iv. 4, 5. Rom. x. 4. 1 Cor. ix. 21. Rom. vii. 6.

Thus it appears, that the *law* was given for ends *subservient* to the *gospel;* and not

U

to *oppose* and *destroy* the gospel. For
which end the corrupt nature of man
doth perversly use it, in endeavouring to
obey it for *righteousness* unto *life*, when
there can be no life had thereby. Not
but that the promise of *life*, upon the
creature's *obedience*, is contained in the
law; as the threatening of *death* on his
disobedience: *For Moses describeth the righ-*
teousness which is of the law, that the man
that doth those things, shall live by them;
as the apostle declares, Rom. x. 5. But
then the *sinner* has already broken the law,
and lost his *power* to fulfil it; and on
both accounts, it is impossible for *him*
to obtain *life* by it: and to *attempt* the
same, is a *God*-dishonouring, and a *soul*-
destroying thing. The soul that seeks
life by the law, *dishonours* God, in that
it does its utmost to *oppose* the great *design*
of his infinite wisdom and grace, in saving sinners by his Son: and it *destroys* itself, in seeking the *blessing* in such a way,
wherein it is impossible to be had; and
whereby it must inevitably fall under the
curse. And such a soul, in *doing* for life,
runs quite counter to God's way of *believ-*
ing for life: and *he that believeth not the*

Son, (living and dying in that state) *shall not see life; but the wrath of God abideth on him*, John iii. 36. which will sink him into the abyss of unutterable and e-ternal torment. But it may be said,

' You talk of *doing* for *life*, and *trust-*
' *ing* to our own obedience for *acceptance*
' with God, and that this is a *soul*-de-
' stroying thing: But who is there that
' goes about it? Do not all that profess
' the name of *Christ*, believe that he died
' to *save* mankind? But we must not
' from thence sit *still*, and do nothing
' *ourselves;* we must do what we *can*, and
' what we cannot *do*, Christ will make up
' by his merit, and God will *forgive* us
' our sins.'

And so the person that makes this ob-jection, would not be thought to *seek life by the works of the law;* but is for salvation in a *mixed* way, partly by *works*, and partly by *grace*. But as no such thing can be, for grace and works, in the point of *salvation*, can no more *mix* than *iron and clay;* so the person that seeks life at *all*, by his own works, will be found to seek it *wholly* by the works of the law, if what Paul says is true, Rom. xi. 6. *And*

if by grace, *then it is no more of works;
otherwise grace is no more grace: but if it
be of works, then is it no more grace; otherwise work is no more work.* It muſt be
wholly of works, or *wholly* of grace. And
therefore every man muſt ſtand either on
the ſide of *works,* or on the ſide of *grace.*
And as it is God's way to ſave ſinners
alone by his *free grace;* ſo every ſoul that
ſhall be ſaved, is made willing to be ſaved
in *this* way. And that ſoul that is not
willing to have ſalvation alone by God's
free grace in Chriſt, without the leaſt regard to his own *works,* in point of *acceptance,* muſt for ever go without it. And
as for that ſoul, whoever he be, that adheres, in the leaſt, to his own *works,* he
will be found to be *of* the works of the
law; and as ſuch, muſt inevitably fall
under the *curſe:* for he, adhering to the
law, chooſes to ſtand at its *bar;* and *that*
requiring of him perfect *obedience,* which
he cannot perform, (although it is his
duty) it will *curſe* him to death for the
want of it. Such a ſoul, in attempting
to do *any* thing for life, tacitly ſays, that
he is able to keep the *whole* law; and ſo
out of his own mouth will be *judged*

and *condemned* for the non-performance of it.

Little do souls know, what a dreadful *task* they undertake, when they go about *working for life*, and to *establish their own righteousness*. They reject the great, full, and free *salvation* of God in the *gospel*, and bind themselves over to the *condemnation* of a broken *law*, and to the fiery *indignation* of a fin-revenging God; and will find it a most *fearful thing to fall* into his *hands*. And whoever thou art, soul, that art for *doing* for life, thou wilt find *enough* to do; for no less than to fulfil the *whole* law doth God *require* of thee thereby. But it may be further said;

' Why, then, we may even *throw* a-
' way the *law*, cast off *subjection* to it,
' and live as we *list*.'

But, hold, man; thou art *under* the law, and canst not so easily deliver thyself from its *yoke*. It bids thee *do*, and do *perfectly:* and though thou canst not yield such an obedience as it requires, yet thou art indispensibly bound to do what thou *canst ;* (yea, and infinitely more than is in thy power to perform) and thou oughtest to do thy utmost, as a *creature*, in point of *obedience* to God, thy Creator and Preserver. And he will regard the acts of thy moral righteousness; and, in the bounties of his providence, *reward* thy obedience, with good things, in this present life. So that, in this respect, thou wilt not serve an hard master: For *whatsoever good thing any man doth, the same shall he receive of the Lord, whether he be bond or free*, Eph. iv. 8. And hence there is *encouragement* enough for *fallen* man, to use his utmost *diligence* to do what God requires of him in his *law*. But if he would be *saved*, he must seek salvation in another *way*; even in that way wherein God has declared it may be had.

For, if a sinful creature, will obey the *law*, with an eye to make himself *righteous* in the sight of God, and to obtain eternal *life* thereby; as this was not God's *end* in giving the *law* to fallen man, so he will say to such an one, *Who hath required these things at your hands?* And cast all his *obedience* as *dung*, and abominable *filth*, into his face, to his everlasting *shame* and utter *confusion:* for, in point of *righteousness* before God, nothing less than

perfect *obedience* can be *accepted;* which a
fallen creature cannot perform: and God
having *appointed* the *obedience* of his Son,
to be the only justifying *righteousness* of a
sinner; if a sinful creature sets aside the
perfect obedience of Christ, by introducing
his own *imperfect* obedience in the stead
thereof; or presents his own *filthy rags;*
to join with Christ's spotless, glorious *robe,*
in order to obtain *life* by the *works* of his
own hands, when God has declared, that
it is only to be had by his *free gift;* it is
a most daring affront to the *grace* of God
in the *gospel,* and to the *justice* of God in
the *law.* And the *condemnation* of such
a soul, will be exceedingly more aggra-
vated, and his *punishment* more intollerable,
that thus adheres to the *law,* under the
promulgation of the *gospel,* than that of
the *heathens* who perish, not having heard
of the *Name* of Christ. And thus it is a
dreadful thing, for a poor sinner, to attempt to *do* any thing himself, that so he
may *inherit eternal* life. For, if *he will
enter into life* that way, he must *keep all
the commandments,* in heart, lip, and life,
without the least failure continually, which
he can never *do;* and so runs himself upon

the flaming Sword of God's *justice*, in his fiery *law;* and dying in that state, he must *suddenly be destroyed, and that without remedy.*   But again, it may be said;

  ' If there is no such thing, as life to
' be had for a fallen creature, by its
' own obedience to the law, then it is
' made void.'

  I answer, with the apostle, *Do we then make void the law through faith? God forbid: yea, we establish the law,* Rom. iii. 31.   It is *those* destroy the *law,* who would put it off with their own *imperfect* obedience: for thereby, they tacitly say, that the *law* is not so strict and holy as it once was; nor so binding to the creature, either in its requirements of duty, or obligation to punishment, as it was wont to be.   But as for *those* who assert, that the law of God is an eternal rule of righteousness, and that it indispensibly requires of every man that is under it, as a covenant of works, perfect and perpetual obedience, which is the creature's duty to perform, although he cannot do it; and that upon default hereof, it righteously binds the transgressor over to punishment, and so set it *aside,* and cease to *obey* it for life; these *establish the law:* in that they, by faith, take hold of Christ's *obedience,* who has fulfilled it perfectly, and is become the *end of it for righteousness, to every one that believeth;* and in that, to all unbelievers who remain under it, they assert its equity and eternity, in requiring of them complete, and constant obedience, and binding them over to death, both in soul and body, in time and to eternity, for the non-performance thereof.

Thus, as it is the *duty* of the creature, man, to *do* whatever his Creator commands in his holy law, which yet he *cannot* do: so it appears to be utterly *impossible* for him to be *justified* by his own o-bedience; and the *misery* of man, with regard to the *law,* is exceeding great indeed: and therefore, the good news the *gospel* brings must needs be *glad tidings;* as it reveals pardon and life for a *sinner,* through the complete *obedience* of Jesus Christ, *imputed* to him for his justifying *righteousness* before God, which is to be received by *faith* alone.

X

****

SECT. VII.
The CONCLUSION.

ISA. xlv. 24.

Surely, shall one say, In the Lord have I righteousness.

IN the last place, I shall add something by way of *use* from what has been said, as a conclusion of the whole. And,

1. Since the *justification* of a sinner is by the complete *obedience* of Jesus Christ, *imputed* to him, and received by *faith*, and produceth such great and glorious *effects*; we may hence learn, what reason we have to *admire* that infinity of *wisdom*, which shines forth in the *contrivance* of this wonder; and to adore that immensity of *grace* which is displayed in this glorious *provision* made for the favourites of

heaven *! When the beloved John was favoured with a visionary fight of the the *woman-bride, the Lamb's wife*, as *clothed with* Christ, *the Sun* of righteousness,

---

* This divine righteousness of the adorable Redeemer, which is the alone ground of a guilty finner's juftification, has many ingredients in it, and peculiar excellencies appertaining to it, that should excite wonder and admiration in these who have had it imputed unto them. It is not only in itself, a full, fufficient, complete, and meritorious righteousness; but a righteousness of God's contrivance, Pfal. lxxxix. 19, 20. Ifa. xlii. 6, 7.;—of God's working out, Heb. ii. 17. John xvii. 4, 19, 30.;—of God's approving, Ifa. xlii. 21.;—of God's accepting, Eph. v. 2.;—of God's revealing, Rom. i. 17. iii. 21.;—of God's bringing near, Heb. ix. 23, 24. Ifa. xlvi. 13.:———But it is alfo a righteousness by which the law is magnified, Ifa. xlii. 21.;—juftice fatisfied, Rom. viii. 34. Pfalm lxxxv. 10.;—fin expiated, Heb. i. 3. ix. 26.;—tranfgreffion finifhed, Dan. ix. 24.—wrath appeafed, and deliverance from it obtained, Micah vii. 18. 1 Theff. i. 10.;—the curfe removed, Gal. iii. 13.;—the guilty affoiled, Rom. viii. 33, 34.;—freedom from condemnation fecured, Rom. viii. 1.;—the finner eternally faved, Ifa. xlv. 17.;—Heaven purchafed, Heb. x. 19, 20.;—God glorified, Ifa. xlix. 3. John xvii. 4.;—Chrift honoured, Ifa. liii. 12. Phil. ii. 8, 9.;—believers adorned and exalted, Isaiah lxi. 10. Pfalm lxxxix. 16.:———And, to crown all, it is a permanent and an everlafting righteousness, Dan. ix. 24. Ifaiah xlv. 17.———What reafon then have the redeemed ones to be filled with wonder and admiration in contemplating the finifhed furety-righteousness!

---

and shining forth in the resplendent rays
of her Bridegroom's glory; he says, he
saw *a* WONDER, Rev. xii. 1. And a wonder it is indeed; so great, that it calls
for the admiration both of men and of
angels. This is one of those glorious
things, that by the gospel is revealed unto
us, *Which the angels desire to look into,*
1 Pet. i. 12. And while sinful men have
the forgiveness of their *sins, through* Christ's
blood, and the *acceptation* of their *persons,*
in him *the Beloved, according to the riches
of* the Father*'s grace, wherein he has a-
bounded towards* them, *in all wisdom and
prudence;* it becomes them to admire, and
adore the same, and to cry out, with the
apostle, *O the depth of the riches, both of
the wisdom and knowledge of God! How
unsearchable are his judgments, and his ways
past finding out!* Eph. i. 6, 7, 8. Rom.
xi. 33. That the *obedience* of the Son of
God should be made our *righteousness,* the
righteousness of a *sinner,* to his complete
justification before God, is such a *project* of
infinite *wisdom,* such a *provision* of infinite
grace, for the *salvation* of God's chosen,
that it every way becomes the great Je-

HOVAH! And will be the endlefs wonder
of men and angels!

2. Since the juftification of a finner is
wholly by the righteoufnefs of another,
which is a *way of life above* nature, above
being difcovered by nature's *light*, and
feen by nature's *eye*, or difcovered by the
light of the *law*, and difcerned by natural *reafon;* we may hence learn, what
an abfolute neceffity there is of a fuper-
natural *revelation* thereof, in order to the
foul's receiving of this *righteoufnefs*, and
fo of the grace of *juftification* thereby.
This is one of thofe *things* that God has
prepared for his people, that never *entered
into the heart of* the natural *man to conceive
of*, which he has neither *known* nor *can*
underftand; and therefore deems it *foolifh-
nefs*, or a foolifh thing, for any to think
they fhall be juftified by the obedience of
Chrift, exclufive of all their own works.
But the people of God, *receive not the
fpirit which is of the world, but the Spirit
which is of God, that they may know the
things which are freely given* them *of God*.
And *this*, of *the free gift of righteoufnefs,
is revealed unto* them by his *Spirit*, though
it is one of thofe *deep things of God*, which

are hidden from the *natural man;* and which are impoffible to be known by any, but heaven-born fouls, under a fpecial *revelation* from above, 1 Cor. ii. 6, *&c.*

3. Since the *juftification* of a finner is by the *obedience* of Chrift alone; we may hence learn, how greatly *important* the *knowledge* thereof is! The *knowledge* of this righteoufnefs, muft needs be of the utmoft *importance,* fince *ignorance* of it, and *non-fubmiffion* to it, (which always go together) leave the foul in an *unrighteous* ftate, Rom. ix. 31, 32. and x. 3. All thofe miferable fouls, who are *ignorant* of Chrift's *righteoufnefs, go about to eftablifh their own righteoufnefs;* and, alas! *The bed is fhorter, than that a man can ftretch himfelf upon it, and the covering narrower, than that he can wrap himfelf in it,* Ifa. xxviii. 20. There is no true *reft* for a *finner,* from the *works* of its own hands; no *covering* for a *naked* foul, from the *fig-leaves* of its own *righteoufnefs,* though ever fo artfully fewed together. Our Lord told his *difciples,* that *except* their *righteoufnefs did exceed the righteoufnefs of the Scribes and Pharifees, they fhould in no cafe enter into the kingdom of heaven,* Mat. v. 20. Thefe

Scribes and Pharifees were the *zealous*, the *religious* men of that *age*, the ftrict obfervers of Mofes's law, that trufted in *themfelves*, that they were *righteous*, by their own *legal* performances, and thought to get to *heaven* by means thereof.   But our Lord declares, that none fhall ever come *there*, but thofe who have a *better* righteoufnefs, a *righteoufnefs* that exceeds a *pharifaical* righteoufnefs; *i. e.* fuch a righteoufnefs, that every way anfwers to all the extenfive requirements of the *law*, in heart, lip, and life; and this is no other than the *righteoufnefs* of Chrift, imputed to poor *finners*, or made *theirs* by *imputation;* in which, being completely *juftified*, according to *law* and *juftice*, they fhall, as *righteous* perfons, be admitted into the kingdom of *heaven*, or into the glory of the heavenly *ftate;* while all thofe who truft in their own *righteoufnefs*, and think they have done *many wonderful works*, which they dare plead for acceptance with God, fhall be fent away from Chrift, into eternal *mifery*, with a *depart from me, ye workers of iniquity*, Matth. vii. 22.

And as our Lord, in this his *fermon*

upon the *mount*, had been expounding
the law of God, in its *spirituality*, as ex-
tending to the *heart*, as well as *life;* and
afferting the neceffity of *keeping* the commandments, in the fame extenfive manner, that the law *required*, in order to
make a perfon *righteous;* fo, in the con-
clufion thereof, he fays, *Therefore, whofoever heareth thefe fayings of mine, and doth
them, I will liken him unto a wife man, who
built his houfe upon a rock: and the rain
defcended and the floods came, and the winds
blew, and beat upon that houfe; and it fell
not, for it was founded upon a rock*, verfes
24, 25. Thefe *fayings* of our Lord, contain the *fubftance* of the moral *law*, and
the *doing* of them unto *righteoufnefs* before
God, is by *believing;* as faith lays hold
on Chrift, who has *obeyed* the law perfectly, as the *reprefentative* of his people: on
which account, *they* may be faid to have
done, or *fulfilled*, the law in him; his
obedience, being *imputed* unto *them*, for
their complete *juftification* before God.

As the *Surety's payment*, among men,
is accounted to the *debtor*, and is the fame,
in the eye of the *law*, and as effectual for
his full *difcharge*, as if he himfelf had

paid the *debt*. And he that thus *doth* the law, or thefe *sayings* of Chrift, he *likens* him *unto a wife man, who built his houfe upon a rock.* It is a piece of natural *wifdom*, to lay a good *foundation* for a ftately *ftructure;* and the moft *firm*, that any houfe can be built on, is that of a *rock*. And he that is fpiritually *wife, wife unto falvation*, lays the whole *ftrefs* of it, and builds all his *hope* of life, upon Chrift, the *rock* of ages; in which it appears, that he is *wife* indeed: for, as in nature, a *houfe* that is built upon a *rock*, will ftand the *ftorm;* fo the *foul* that is built upon *Chrift* fhall never be *removed: the rain may defcend, the floods come, and the winds beat ;* afflictions, temptations, and trials of all kinds, may *beat vehemently againft* that foul; but fhall never *deftroy* its *falvation*, nor make it *afhamed* of its *hope*. No; Chrift, the *rock* of immutability, will hold it *unfhaken*, in a ftate of *falvation*, through *life*, through *death*, at *judgment*, and *for ever*.—Such a foul *ftands* as *immoveable*, in the grace of *juftification* and *life*, as the *rock* itfelf on which it is founded: *Becaufe I live*, faith our Lord, *ye fhall live alfo*, John xiv. 19. Chrift's

Y

life is the life of that *foul*, that depends upon him alone, for all its justification, and eternal falvation.   And therefore the *wifdom* of faith is great indeed! in that it forefees the ftorm, and thus provids a-gainft it.

But he, faith our Lord, *that heareth thefe fayings of mine, and doth them not* [*i. e.* that *heareth* the law's *requirements*, and endeavours to *obey* the fame, for *righteoufnefs* before God, and fo doth them *not*; becaufe his obedience cannot come up to that perfection which the law requires] *fhall be likened unto a foolifh man, which built his houfe upon the fand; and the rain defcended, and the floods came, and the winds blew, and beat upon that houfe; and it fell, and great was the fall of it,* Matth. vii. 26; 27,   Oh! the *folly* of that poor finner, who lays the *ftrefs* of his falvation, and builds his *hope* of life, upon his *own* righteoufnefs!   For this *fandy* foundation cannot endure the *ftorms* of divine *wrath*, which fhall be revealed from heaven againft all unrighteoufnefs of men; nor fecure the foul from being driven away, by the tempeft of God's *anger*, and the floods of his *indignation*, into the abyfs of eternal *mifery.* The *houfe fell,* that was thus built upon the *fand, and great was the fall of it!* Oh! what a miferable difappointment will it be to that foul, that *goes down to the chambers of* eternal *death, with this lie of his own righteoufnefs in his right-hand;* from which he had all along hoped for eternal life! When this *way, that feemed right to him in his own eyes,* as if it would lead him to everlafting life, (by his *depending* thereon) fhall *end* in eternal *death! The hope of the hypocrite* [or, of him that trufts in himfelf, that he is righteous, by his own external performances, when yet his heart is far from that conformity to God, which the law *requires*] *fhall perifh, at the giving up of the ghoft.* His *hope* [i. e. his *falvation* hoped for] *fhall* then *be cut off. He fhall lean upon his houfe,* [i. e. his own *righteoufnefs,* which he had raifed up, in his imagination, to *fhelter* him from the *ftorm* of divine vengeance] *but it fhall not ftand; he fhall hold it faft, but it fhall not endure,* Job viii. 13, 14, 15. No; this *houfe* of his fhall be as foon deftroyed, by the ftorm of God's indignation, as a *fpider's web* is fwept down by the befom that comes againſt it; and the miſerable ſoul, that truſted herein, ſhall be driven away into eternal perdition.

Thus an error in the *foundation* will prove *fatal* to the building; and therefore the *knowledge* of *Chriſt*, as the alone way of a ſinner's *juſtification* and *life*, muſt needs be of the higheſt *importance;* ſince no other *refuge* can ſtand the *ſtorm*, but Chriſt, as THE LORD OUR RIGHTEOUSNESS; this glorious *hiding-place* which God has prepared for poor ſinners, whither they may *run*, and be for ever *ſafe*. And as for *thoſe*, who live and die in *ignorance* of, and *non-ſubmiſſion to* the righteouſneſs of Chriſt, they will certainly *die in their ſins*, and *periſh* for ever. They will all be found *filthy* at the day of judgment, that have not been enabled to *believe* in Chriſt's *blood*, for cleanſing from all ſin; they will all be found *unjuſt*, at that awful day, that have not *believed* in the Redeemer's *righteouſneſs*, for their juſtification before God; and ſo muſt remain *for ever:* for, concerning them, it will then be ſaid, *He that is filthy, let him be filthy ſtill; and he that is unjuſt, let him be unjuſt ſtill;*

i. e. let him *abide* so to an endless *eternity.* But,

4. Since there is but one *way* for a sinner to be *justified* before God, and that is by the *obedience* of Christ alone; this informs us, what great *folly* those persons are guilty of, who *press* poor sinners to obey the *law*, to make themselves *righteous* in the sight of God, when there is no law given that can give life unto them; and how *dangerous* it is for souls, to sit under such a ministry, that naturally *misleads* them; since, while *the blind leads the blind, both fall into the ditch. If there had been a law given that could have given life,* says the apostle, *verily righteousness should have been by the law*, Gal. iii. 21. But as there is no law given, that can give life to a sinner, it is a *vain, foolish* thing, to *press* such a soul, to get a *righteousness* by his own *performances*, which was never appointed of God, nor can be *attained* by man. No; *the scripture hath concluded all under sin, that the promise* (of life) *by faith of Jesus Christ* (as a sinner's righteousness) *might be given to them that believe*, verse 22. And those who receive it not in this *way*, shall never attain it in

any *other*, but muſt go *without* it for ever. *The labour of the fooliſh*, ſays the **wiſe man**, *wearieth every one of them, becauſe he knoweth not how to go to the city*, Ecclef. x. 15. A man may labour all his *days*, to make himſelf *righteous* before God, by his own *performances*, and to make his *peace* with him, by his *legal* repentance, and humiliation for *ſin*; and yet *loſe* all his labour at *laſt*, and ſo weary himſelf in *vain*, being never able to reach that *city*, that eternal reſt, which God has prepared for his people: becauſe he *knoweth* not *Chriſt*, the only *way*, that leads thither; and ſo *walks* not by faith, in him, as ſuch.

All men by nature, are ignorant of Chriſt's *righteouſneſs*, as it is God's *way* of *juſtifying* and *ſaving* a finner; and it is *dangerous* for fouls to fit under ſuch a miniſtry, that preſſeth *doing*, and perſuades them their *ſafety* lies there, inſtead of *believing*: for, *how ſhall they believe*, ſaith the apoſtle, *in him of whom they have not heard? and how ſhall they hear without a preacher? And how ſhall they preach, except they be ſent?* Rom. x. 14, 15. How ſhall poor fouls *believe* in Chriſt for *justification,* when they have never heard of his *righteousness,* which is the proper *object* of faith? And how shall they *hear,* without a *preacher* of that gospel which declares it? And how shall they *preach* the gospel to others, who have never *seen* that salvation it reveals for sinners, by the *righteousness* of Christ themselves? How shall they declare the glory and efficacy thereof to *others,* who have never seen, nor experienced it *themselves?* And how does it appear, that they are *sent* by Christ, to preach the gospel, who neither *know,* nor *proclaim* his *righteousness,* for the *justification* of a sinner, which is such a main *doctrine* thereof?

Have we not reason to fear, that many of those who are called *ministers* of the *gospel,* are rather *preachers* of *Moses,* than of *Christ?* and that their *ministry* rather tends to lead souls to the bondage and death of the *law,* than to the liberty and life of the *gospel?* But, *how beautiful are the feet of them that preach the gospel of peace, that bring glad tidings of good things!* That publish that *peace* with God, which was made for sinners alone, by the *blood* of Christ's cross; and is possest, only by *faith* in him! That proclaim the glad tidings of thofe good things, which God has prepared to be enjoyed by *finners,* through the juftifying *righteoufnefs* of his Son! And how great is the privilege of thofe fouls, who fit under a *gofpel*-miniftry; fince this is the *means* appointed of God, to work *faith* in them, and to bring *falvation* to them! Once more,

5. Since the *juftification* of a finner is by the *righteoufnefs* of Chrift, *imputed* to him, and received by *faith* alone; we may hence learn, how great the *obligation* of the *juftified* ones is, to *live* to the *glory* of that *grace*, which has fo freely and fully *juftified* them, in and through Chrift, unto eternal *life* by him! When the apoftle had afferted the juftification and falvation of God's people, both *Jews* and *Gentiles*, to be wholly of his free *mercy*, in and through Chrift, Rom. xi. 32. and admired the riches of his *wifdom*, which was fo brightly difplayed in the difpenfations of his *mercy* towards them, verfe 33. he thus concludes his difcourfe, verfe 36. *For of him, and through him, and to him are all things; to whom be glory for ever,* Amen. It is as if he fhould fay, fince all

things, relating to the juſtification and ſalvation of God's people, are *of* him, and *through* him, it is meet that the glory of all ſhould, by them, be given *to* him: and therefore, when he applies this doctine of God's free mercy in Chriſt, to them who had obtained it, he thus addreſſeth them, chap. xii. 1. *I beſeech you therefore, brethren, by the mercies of God, that ye preſent your bodies a living ſacrifice, holy, acceptable unto God, which is your reaſonable ſervice.* I beſeech *you*, ſays he; *You* that have obtained *mercy; therefore,* or, ſince it is God's deſign, to *glorify* his mercy, in the ſalvation of ſinners, that you give him the *glory* of it: *by the mercies of God;* thoſe *mercies* of God, which you are partakers of, in the *forgiveneſs* of all your *ſins,* and in the *juſtification* of your *perſons; that ye preſent your bodies a living ſacrifice, holy, acceptable unto God,* that ye continually offer up yourſelves, as a whole burnt-offering, in the flames of *love,* unto him that hath *loved* you, in all holy and acceptable *obedience,* to the *glory* of that God, who has thus had *mercy* upon you; *which is your reaſonable ſervice,* for it is a moſt reaſonable thing, or a thing

Z

for which there is the higheſt *reaſon*, that you ſhould ever *ſerve* the Lord, to the *glory* of that *grace*, by which you are freely *juſtified*, and ſhall be eternally *glorified*. And thus the apoſtle Peter, 1 Pet. ii. 9. *But ye are a choſen generation, a royal prieſt-hood,* [who are waſhed from all your ſins in Chriſt's blood, and clothed with his righteouſneſs] *an holy nation, a peculiar people ; that ye ſhould ſhew forth the praiſes of him who hath called you out of darkneſs, into his marvelous light.* And, *you know,* ſays the apoſtle Paul, *how we exhorted and comforted, and charged every one of you,* [*i. e.* of you juſtified, ſaved ones] *that ye would walk worthy of God, who hath called you unto his kingdom and glory,* 1 Theſſ. ii. 11, 12.

And in ſhort, as it was God's deſign to get himſelf *glory*, in the *juſtification* of ſinners, by the *righteouſneſs* of Jeſus Chriſt; ſo the *diſplay* thereof, throughout the whole goſpel, lays *them* under the higheſt *obligation* to *live* to his *praiſe*. Does God the *Father impute* the *obedience* of his Son to poor ſinners? Did God the *Son obey*, in *life* and in *death* for them? And does God the *Spirit, reveal* and *apply* this righ-

teousness to them, and enable them to *receive* the same, as a *free gift* of grace, unto their eternal *life* in glory? What thanks, what praise, is due to God, in each of his glorious persons, for this abundant grace! And let the language of the justified ones, in heart, lip, and life, in all kinds of holy *obedience*, both now, and always be, *Thanks be unto God, for the grace of* JUSTIFICATION! *for this, his unspeakable* GIFT! 2 Cor. ix. 15. *Amen! Hallelujah!*

THE END.

ERRATA.

Preface, p. viii. l. 9, 10. for *imminent*, read *immanent*.
p. x. l. 5. from the foot, for *addition*, read *edition*.

APPENDIX.*

AS no revealed truth is of greater importance to the sons of men, than the justification of a guilty sinner, through the imputed righteousness of Christ; so, there can be no inquiry more interesting than for a person to know, if they be divorced from the law, as a covenant; married to Christ, as their best husband; and clothed with the robe of his justifying righteousness, as their adorning garment. To attain some satisfaction on this important point, the conscience may be posed with the following questions, as an additional improvement of the foregoing subject.

1. Did you ever come to *yourselves?* Luke xv. 17.; that is, did you ever feel yourselves to be bound with the cords of guilt, laden with iniquity, and ready to sink into the bottomless pit? Men must be condemned, before they are justified; be cast down, before they are lifted up; apply the curse to themselves, before they take hold of the blessing; hear the sentence of death denounced against them by the law, before they partake of the justification of life by the gospel.—If you were never burdened, you cannot be eased; if you were never broken, you cannot be bound up; if you were never mourners, you cannot be comforted; if you never tasted the bitterness of sin, you cannot taste of the sweetness of the grace of Christ, and experience his pu-

* This Appendix was not in the first impression of this Book.

rifying blood, and his reviving righteousness.—If you are justified, how did you come by pardon and peace? Was it by wrestling and prayer?

2. Are you *sanctified?* Justification and sanctification always go together. Where ever the blood of Christ is applied to justify, his Spirit is implanted to sanctify: they are always joined together, John xix. 34. Blood and water came out of his side; blood to justify, and water to sanctify. Jesus, at the same time that he satisfied for sin, crucified our *old man*, Rom. iv. 6. Those who are justified, by the sprinkling of his blood, are also redeemed from all iniquity, and consecrated to God. Where Christ washes with his blood, he likewise anoints with his Spirit.

3. Are we *adopted?* Justification is always attended with adoption. These who receive the *white stone* of justification, from all their sins, have also in it the *new name*, Rev. ii. 17. What is this new name, but the name of a child of God? Adoption is an amplification of our justification. We are not only pronounced righteous, and owned as friends; but reputed and accepted as sons and daughters; are nearly related, and greatly endeared to God.

4. Do you *love* God and Christ? It is recorded concerning Mary, *That she loved much, because much was forgiven her*, Luke vii. 47. When great debts are remitted, heinous sins pardoned, deep spots and stains fetched out, this calls for the highest and most fervent love. It is said, Prov. xvii. 9. *He that covereth transgression, seeketh love.* Surely then, with the greatest propriety it may be said, that God and Christ have sought our love, by *covering our sins*, Psalm xxxii. 1, 2. If you give not your hearts to God, if you do not set your love on Christ, who redeems from all iniquity, it is a plain sign that you have not tasted of the grace of God, or experienced the kindness of Christ in forgiving your sins.

5. What free *access* have you to God, and what joy and delight have you in him? Are your consciences so perfectly purged from iniquity, that you dare draw nigh God with confidence and boldness? *Having therefore, brethren, boldness to enter into the holiest by the blood of Jesus*, Heb. vii. 19. and x. 19. Do you rejoice in God, through Christ Jesus our Lord, as having now *received the atonement?* Rom. v. 11. Are you so justified in the Lord as to glory? Isa. xlv. 25. *In the Lord shall all the seed of Israel be justified, and shall glory.* Is your justification matter of the greatest joy to you? *I will greatly rejoice in the Lord, my soul shall be joyful in my God; for he hath covered me with the robe of righteousness*, Isaiah lxi. 10.

6. Are you employed, and do you take great pleasure and delight to *bless* and *praise* the Lord, for pardoning all your sins, and reconciling you to himself? This was David's delightful employment; *Bless the Lord, O my soul; and all that is within me bless his holy name,—who forgiveth all mine iniquities*, Psalm ciii. 1, 2, 3. Justified souls will sing praises to God who heals their backslidings; and rejoice in Christ Jesus, who is their righteousness and ransom: The redeemed of the Lord shall return to *Zion with songs*, Isa. xxxv. 10. Our lips were once sealed up with guilt; but now the mouths of accusers are stoped, by Christ's satisfaction: and shall not our lips then be opened, and our tongues loosed, to sing aloud of God's grace, and of Christ's righteousness?

7. Are you willing to go out of this world; to *die*, and to be with God, and Jesus Christ? Those that are justified have *peace with God*, and *rejoice in the hope of the glory of God*, Rom. v. 1, 2. Though condemned sinners shall be cast away on the shores of a miserable eternity; yet justified souls shall be landed safe in the harbour of glory, and enjoy a blessed eternity. When others pass into the prison

of hell, juftified perfons enter into the palace of God, Matth. xxv. 34, 41. When the tares are reaped for the furnace, believers are reaped for, and gathered into the garner, Matth. iii. 12.—Will juftified perfons fhun the glorious prefence of God, and flavifhly dread his tribunal? Will pardoned and adopted perfons be afraid to go home to their Father, and be put in poffeffion of the heavenly inheritance? Are you therefore willing to be *abfent from the* body, and to be *prefent with the Lord*, 2 Cor. v. 6, 8. Can you therefore conquer the fears of death? are you willing to leave your place on earth, to enjoy the place prepared for you in heaven? to put off the rags of mortality, that you may be clothed with the robes of glory? to quit your *earthly tabernacle, for the boufe not made with hands eternal in the heavens?* 2 Cor. v. 1.

If thefe, and the like, are your attainments, and the happy difpofitions of your foul, they may be viewed as fo many infallible evidences, that you have paffed from death to life, are in a juftified ftate, interefted in the Redeemer's righteoufnefs, have it imputed unto you, and fhall, in due time, be honoured to *fee God's face in righteoufnefs*, Pfalm xvii. 15.

As thefe are the only *happy* perfons who have the righteoufnefs of Chrift imputed to them, and are *made the righteoufnefs of God in him*, 2 Cor. v. 21.; fo they are of all others the moft *miferable* who have no intereft therein.——Why, they are in their *natural* ftate, and the fcripture defcribes all fuch not only to be *ftout-hearted* and *far from righteoufnefs*, Ifa. xlvi. 12; but to be *filled with all unrighteoufnefs*, Rom. i. 29.——Thefe who are not juftified have all their *fins recorded* in God's book, Ifa. lxv. 6. Man's iniquity is faid to be written, fo as to be marked before God, Jer. ii. 22.; and there is a counterpart of this record kept in the finner's own confcience, Jer.

xvii. r.—Till Chrift becomes their righteoufnefs, their fouls are *fhamefully naked*, Rev. iii. 17. As men are poor, they are void of an inherent righteoufnefs; and, as they *are naked*, they are deftitute of an imputed righteoufnefs. Till the righteoufnefs of Chrift is fpread over the foul, the glorious image of God is not put on it.—Till they are juftified, there is a *breach* between God and them. Sin hath made a breach; and this breach ftands open, and we need a Mediator to ftand in the gap, Pfalm cvi. 23. But there is none fit for this, but Jefus Chrift, the living advocate, 1 John ii. 1.—There is a dreadful *ftorm of wrath*, in the cloud of the threatenings, which hangs over the heads of guilty finners, Pfalm xi. 6. This cup of indignation fhall come to their lips; this ftorm fhall fall on their fouls. If God rains, the ftorm muft needs be terrible: *I will rain*, fays Jehovah, Gen. vii. 4. Though, by reafon of unbelief, *God's judgments are now far above, out of the fight of finners*, Pfalm x. 5.; yet *their eyes fhall fee their deftruction*, and *they fhall drink of the wrath of the Almighty*, Job xxi. 20. The long and large roll of the curfe will in due time fly to them, Ezek. lii. 2, 3, 4.——All the fins of unjuftified perfons are fo many *evidences* and *witneffes* againft them: thefe evidences are preferved and kept fafe; their fins are hid that they may not be loft, Hof. xiii. 12. *The iniquity of Ephraim is bound up, his fin is hid.* Their iniquity is bound up, that in due time it may be bound on them; their fin is fo hid, that it fhall be found, brought forth, and charged on them. So many fins as men have committed, and are unpardoned, fo many witneffes have they provided againft the day of their trial, Jer. xiv. 7. *O Lord, our iniquities teftify againft us.* Ifa. lix. 12.—— Every fin deferves, and every unjuftified foul will be rewarded with *eternal death*, Rom. vi. 23. Death is ὀ ϕ ὠντα, the *wages of fin*. The word fignifies *soldiers wages,* Luke iii. 14. They who cleave to Satan as their general, who abide in his tents, fight on his side against God, shall have eternal death as wages paid them, Isaiah lix. 18. and liv. 15. And as there is a judgment to come, God, who seeth the provocations of all men, will be a *swift witness against them,* Matth iii 5. And if their sins are not pardoned, but remain before God's face, and they inherit the iniquities of their whole life, they will be heirs of shame, misery, and eternal torments, Psalm xc. 8. Job xiii. 26. *The wicked shall be turned into hell.*

Though this be the unhappy situation of all unjustified persons, who have no interest in the Redeemer's righteousness; yet, such is the goodness of God to poor sinners, that he *brings near this righteousness* to them, Isaiah xlvi. 13.; he reveals it fully to them in the gospel, for it is the *ministration of righteousness,* 2 Cor. v. 18.: and Christ himself declares, that he is the *end of the law for righteousness to every one that believeth,* Rom. x. 4.; and that *his righteousness is unto and upon all that believe,* Rom. iii. 22.——And all the redeemed shall glory in it, saying, *Surely, in the Lord have I righteousness and strength. In him shall all the seed of Israel be justified, and shall glory,* Isaiah xlv. 24, 25. *I will greatly rejoice in the Lord, my soul shall be joyful in my God; for he hath clothed me with the garments of salvation, he hath covered me with the robe of righteousness,* Isaiah lxi. 10.

F I N I S.

A a

THE
CONTENTS.

A

LIST of the SUBSCRIBERS.

MR. John M'Lachlan, teacher of Mathematics
William Robertson
William Findlay, student
John Walker, student
John Colquhoun, student.
William Bow, student
Robert M'Farlan, student
Wil. Clogston, schoolmaster
Richard Talbot
John M'Naught
John Richardson, student
Alex. Brown
David Ewing, student
Thomas Watson
William Robertson
William M'Vey
John Sorell
Alex. Young
Joseph Hunter
James Allan, 12 copies
Henry Crosby, 12 copies
John Ruthven
John Leckie
William Pinkerton, 12 copies
Robert Person
William Salmon, 7 copies
Robert Brown,
Patrick Houston
James Allan
Alex. Horn, student, 24 copies
William Stevenson
John Irvine
James Chalmers
James M'Indoe
James Gibb
Hugh Watson, 12 copies
John Livingston
John Clark, 12 copies
Hugh Christy
Joseph Pender
Will. White, bookseller, Beith, 60 copies
David Hog
William Boyd

Robert Anderson
John Grant
William Ronald
William M'Dugald
Dugald Dove
William Graham
William Forbes
Edward M'Indoe
John Jack
James Buchanan
William Wilson
James Pollock
William Scott
James M'Gibbon, schoolmaster, 12 copies
John Ferguson, schoolmaster, 8 copies
John M'Keoun
Robert Wilson
David Seth
Andrew Blair
James M'Farlane
Andrew Weir
Thomas Wilkie
Duncan Blair
Daniel M'Gilvra
John Barr
Andrew Aiton
Robert Bethun
William Steel
John M'Farlane
David Doeg, 12 copies
Robert Gentels
John Wright, teacher
Joshua Campbell
John Lochhead
Grizel Richmond
Andrew Dove
James Montieth, student
John Ferguson, 6 copies
William Watson
John M'Lachlan, teacher of Music
John Walker, student
James Fairley, student, 6 copies

SUBSCRIBERS NAMES.

Daniel M'Call, 14 copies
James Stewart,
James Campbell
Michael Cameron
Robert Zuill
Judeth Brody
William Zuill
Hugh M'Dugall
Robert Forrester
Donald M'Lean
William Zuill
John Masson, 2 copies
Mr Anderson, preacher
James M'Indoe
Robert Walker
Patrick Duncan
William Allan
Widow Gardiner
John Grant
Betty Cooper
Archibald Ruthven
Henry M'Dougall, student
John Blair
John Brounlie
William Reid
Walter Stewart
William Reid
William Shaw
Mary Lyle
Rev Mr. William Bell, Minister
    of Campsie
Thomas M'Cuming
Thomas Kerr
William Reid, 12 copies
Walter Craig
William Pinkerton, shoemaker
    24 copies
John Steven
James Morton
Alex. Clyde
Andrew Aloes
Thomas Lees
Malcom Morrison
James M'Call
Robert Thomson
Archibald Cameron
Robert Williamson
John Kerr
Duncan Baxter
James Ferguson
James Stirling

George Wise
Robert Taylor
Alex Cunningham
John M'Ceg, student
Archibald Murdoch, student
James Steven
Robert Peebles
Alex. Humphreys, student
John Morrison
Robert M'Nie
John Gardner
William Simpson, student
Robert M'Gown, mercht. Dum
    barton, 12 copies
William Glen, 6 copies
John Dounie
James Mitchell
Hugh Morrison, student
Samuel Barr, student
Moses Swan, student
Alex Ferguson, 36 copies
John Ferguson
James Ferguson
William Watson
William Hamilton
William Gilfillan
James Baird
James Urie
James Telfer
John Shaw
John M'Dugall
William Atkin
Thomas Graham
John Gardiner,
Duncan M'Farlane
Robert Findlay
Archibald M'Keoun
Angus Betton
Peter M'Lachlan
James Sym
Robert Hamilton
William Rankine
Peter Millar
William Gardiner
James Bennie
Bartholemew Sellers
Donald Taylor, schoolmaster at
    Strachurr
Colin Lamont, schoolmaster at
    Inverchollan
Robert Hamilton

SUBSCRIBERS NAMES.

William Angus
John Rae, 12 copies
James Donaldson
John Coruith
Walter Neilson
David Young
James Stewart
Robert Bulloch
Dougald Buchanan
John M'Gibbon
Alex. Walker
James Ruffel
Isobel Dobie
John Campbell
Thomas Atkin
Thomas Young, merchant, Biggar, 60 copies
Thomas Ritchie
Andrew Ritchie
William Alston
William Houston
James Wilson
John Cook
John Young
James Clark
Thomas Moubray
Andrew Shanks
William Aitken, Biggar, 12 copies
Elizabeth Weir
Agnes Rae
Jean Hog
Andrew Robb
Nichol Porteous
James Ferguson
James Aitken
George Permoin
John Wilson
Alex. Williamson
John Morgan
James Girdwood
William Graham, 12 copies
John M'Ouarg
Thomas Demock
William Simpson
James Jackson
Robert Williamson
John Black, merchant, Biggar, 24 copies
Alex. Inck
John Barclay

Adam Hislop
Thomas Carmichael
William Lawrie
Robert Pairman
John Johnston
William M'Moran
John Masterton
John Lindsay
Robert Brown
John Shanklaw
James Paterson
John Mitchell
John Carrick
William Johnston
John Purdie
Michael Brown
William Ruth
William Lowrie
John Smith
Mr. James Telfer, Carwood
William Gardner, taylor, New Kilpatrick, 48 copies
William Petter
James Ruffel
John Parlane
Robert Brock
Walter Minzies
John Douglas
Daniel Ferguson
Robert Peter
William Harvie
John M'Indoe
James Mason
Walter Graham
John Peter
James Meicklejohn
Hugh M'Gregor
Andrew Crawford
James Bowman
Grame Sinclair
Robert Mitchell
James Peter
James M'Nicol
James Neilson
John Carse
John Moffet
James Provan
James Millar
John M'Nair
John Galbraith
James Millar

SUBSCRIBERS NAMES.

Alex. Muir
James Copeland
John Edmond
Peter Brown
John Clark
George Arpies
William Dun
John Rae
Daniel M'Kenzie
William Zuill
John M'Kellar, teacher, 14 copies
James Forbes
Mrs Wright
William Murray
James Graham
Alex. Ferguson
Thomas Brody
Alex. Campbell
Kenneth M'Callum
Alex. Campbell
Duncan M'Kellar
John Boyd
John M'Farlane
John Smith, merchant, Kilmarnock, 128 copies
John Fleming, wright there, 6 copies
Robert Fleeming, jun.
James Watson
John King
James Crawford
Robert Dunnton
John Fleeming
William Aitken, student
Thomas Smith
Dugald M'Dougall
Andrew White, 25 copies
John Crawford, Kilmarnock, 30 copies
William Brown
John Raeburn
John Gilmour
Andrew Creelmore
William Baird
Thomas Wallace
James Warper
William Brown
Andrew Hutcheson
Andrew Creelmore, jun.
Alex. M'Lean

Thomas Wylie
James Smith
William Newland
Margaret Smith
Agnes Paterson
Jean Morris
Janet Smith
Margaret Steel
Robert Hamilton
James Mitchell
Matthew Burnet
James Aitken
Peter Thomson
Moses Govan
Malcom M'Intosh
John Webb
Mr. Thomson
John Wright
Robert Barrie
Alex. Inch
John Barclay
John Russel
William M'Nicol
James Muir
William Jervey
John Walker
James Graham
James Logan
John Leitch
Walter Bulloch
James Lapslay
Jean Howet
John Buchanan
John Leckie
John M'Nicol
Daniel M'Nicol
Daniel M'Kechnie
John Brash
John M'Nicol
Robert Gardiner
Robert Aitken
Alex. M'Alaster
James M'Murray
John M'Auslan, merchant Greenock, 300 copies
James Colquhoun, student
James Crawford student, 2 copies
Henry M'Nab, student
Samuel Hay, 12 copies
Alex. Kennington
Allan M'Lean

SUBSCRIBERS NAMES.

John Morrifon
Robert M'Nie
Archibald M'Lay
John Gardener
William Simfon
James Hardy
David Steel
Hugh Campbell
Alexander Shaw
John M'Farlane
John Biggar
Thomas Aitken
David Craw
William Broom, merchant, in Dumfries, 54 copies
William Martin, 12 copies
Robert Morton
James Hairftones
John Hairftones
Thomas Johnfton
James Mathie
Thomas Niven
George Morris
George Mitchell

Matthew Mitchell
James M'Keig
John Fergufon
Thomas Gillefpie
Thomas Mitchell
Edward Moffat
Robert Adam
John Egar
Jofeph Broom, merchant, Dumfries, 50 copies
Robert Barr
James Miller, 200 copies
Antony Dempfter
John M'Naughton
Mrs Buchanan
John Livingfton, junior, merchant, in Glafgow
Henry M'Nabb
John Scales
William M'Coul
William Gardener
John Hamilton
Charles Dobby
John Waddal

GLASGOW, *Feb.* 21ft, 1778.

PROPOSALS
For Printing by Subfcription,
A new and handfome Edition of
A
TREATISE
CONCERNING THE
NEW-BIRTH.

To which will be fubjoined,
THIRTY-SIX LETTERS, on Spiritual Subjects, written on divers Occafions; and fent to Relations and Friends.

By the Reverend
Mr. THOMAS DUTTON,
Late Minifter in LONDON.

With a Recommendatory PREFACE, by the Rev. Mr. JACOB ROGERS, B. A.

CONDITIONS.

I. The Book will be printed on a good paper, and elegant type, the fame as the preceding Treatife.

II. It will make about 24 fheets in print, or 384 pages.

III. The price to Subfcribers will be only 2 s. neatly bound, paid on the delivery.

IV. There will be a few copies on a fine paper, at three fhillings, neatly bound.

V. Thofe who fubfcribe for 12 copies, fhall have one *gratis.*

VI. It will be put to the prefs, fo foon as a competent number of fubfcriptions are procured, and finifhed without lofs of time.

*** It is expected that all who wifh to encourage an impreffion of this ufeful Treatife, and Religious Letters, will fubfcribe without delay.

☞ It is quite needlefs to advance any thing here, either in commendation of the Author, or the performances now offered to the public. The preceeding Treatife on JUSTIFICATION, will give the beft Specimen of his abilities and judicious fentiments.

SUBSCRIPTIONS are taken in by A. Coubrough, bookfeller, the Publifher; and W. Smith, Printer, Glafgow; and all others entrufted with Propofals.